D1634916

ESSENTIAL
BARCELONA

Original text by Teresa Fisher
Updated by Suzanne Wales

© Automobile Association Developments Limited 2009
First published 2007
Reprinted 2009. Information verified and updated

ISBN: 978-0-7495-6003-4

Published by AA Publishing, a trading name of Automobile Association Developments
Limited, whose registered office is Fanum House, Basing View, Basingstoke,
Hampshire RG21 4EA. Registered number 1878835.

Colour separation: MRM Graphics Ltd
Printed and bound in Italy by Printer Trento S.r.l.

A03616
Maps in this title produced from mapping © MAIRDUMONT/Falk Verlag 2008
Transport map © Communicarta Ltd, UK

About this book

Symbols are used to denote the following categories:

✚ map reference to maps on cover

✉ address or location

☎ telephone number

🕓 opening times

✋ admission charge

🍴 restaurant or café on premises
or nearby

🚇 nearest underground train station

🚌 nearest bus/tram route

🚉 nearest overground train station

⛴ nearest ferry stop

✈ nearest airport

ℹ tourist information office

❓ other practical information

➤ indicates the page where you will
find a fuller description

This book is divided into six sections.

The essence of Barcelona pages 6–19
Introduction; Features; Food and drink;
Short break including the 10 Essentials

Planning pages 20–33
Before you go; Getting there; Getting
around; Being there

Best places to see pages 34–55
The unmissable highlights of any visit
to Barcelona

Best things to do pages 56–81
Great cafés; stunning views; places to
take the children and more

Exploring pages 82–161
The best places to visit in Barcelona,
organized by area

Excursions pages 161–183
Places to visit out of town

Maps

All map references are to the maps on
the covers. For example, Casa Milà has
the reference ✚ 8F – indicating the grid
square in which it is to be found.

Admission prices

Inexpensive (under €3)
Moderate (€3–€9)
Expensive (over €9)

Hotel prices

Prices are per room per night:
€ budget (under €110);
€€ moderate (€110–€180);
€€€ expensive to luxury (over €180)

Restaurant prices

Price for a three-course meal per person
without drinks:
€ budget (under €20);
€€ moderate (€20–€45);
€€€ expensive (over €45)

Contents

BEST THINGS TO DO

56 – 81

EXPLORING...

82 – 161

EXCURSIONS

162 – 182

The essence of...

Barcelona is unique. It has something for everyone and is one of Europe's top destinations. The only problem you will encounter is that there will never be enough time to explore its many museums and monuments, churches and galleries, its fascinating coastline and its delectable cuisine.

To enjoy your stay to the fullest, you will need to adopt the Barcelonan lifestyle – a striking blend of businesslike efficiency combined with long alfresco lunches, lazy siestas, ritual evening promenades and an intoxicating nightlife. You will long remember its proud yet generous people, who will welcome you back with open arms when you return, as you surely will.

features

Inventive and innovative, radical and racy, Barcelona is one of Europe's most dynamic cities. Strolling through its streets is like wandering through a living museum, a legacy of its remarkable 2,000 years of history. From the ancient maze-like Gothic quarter, built within the Roman city walls, to the astonishing regimental grid plan of the turn-of-the-19th-century Eixample district, studded with eye-catching jewels of Modernista architecture, and the space-age constructions for the 1992 Olympics, the city contains some of the finest and most eccentric art and architecture in the world. Outstanding even by Barcelonan standards is Gaudí's extraordinary Sagrada Família – reason enough to visit the city.

Just as *Modernisme* – the movement that has made Barcelona unique – emerged at the end of the 19th century as a desire for change and renovation, so today the city is celebrating its past.

It is restoring its old buildings, introducing new art and architecture and eradicating some severe urban problems, while staying at the forefront of contemporary culture. As a result, Barcelona today is very much alive – a city bursting with new pride and self-confidence, which cannot fail to excite and delight.

GEOGRAPHY
● Barcelona is in northeastern Spain, 166km (103 miles) from the French border. The city occupies 99sq km (62sq miles), with 13km (8 miles) of Mediterranean coastline, including 4km (2.5 miles) of sandy beaches. It is bounded by the mountains of Montjuïc (to the south) and Tibidabo (to the northwest), and framed by the rivers Llobregat (to the south) and Besós (to the north).

PEOPLE AND ECONOMY
● Barcelona's population is 1,673,075 (or 3,161,081 within the *area metropolitana* of greater Barcelona). Many inhabitants originated from southern Spain, drawn to Catalonia in the 1950s and 1960s by the prospect of work in the capital of Spain's most progressive and prosperous region.

BARCELONA FOR WHEELCHAIR USERS
● Barcelona is a compact city so is a popular destination for wheelchair users, and the modern attractions are wheelchair-friendly. However, many streets are cobbled, which can be uncomfortable unless appropriate tyres are fitted. The *Bus Turístic* has low-entry doors and wheelchair points and all buses are wheelchair accessible. Most major Metro stations are adapted to be suitable for wheelchairs.

CATALUNYA (CATALONIA)
● The autonomous region of Catalunya (Catalonia) covers an area of 31,930sq km (12,325sq miles) (6.3 per cent of Spain) and has a population of around 7 million (15 per cent of the Spanish population), 70 per cent of whom live in greater Barcelona. It is Spain's leading economic region, producing 8 per cent of the country's gross national product. Nearly 40 per cent of all visitors to Spain come to Catalonia.

food & drink

No one visiting Barcelona should leave without trying its cuisine, described by the American food critic Colman Andrews as 'the last great culinary secret in Europe'. Rooted in the fresh local ingredients of the mountains, the plains and sea, the food is delicious and suprisingly subtle in flavour.

MEDITERRANEAN FLAVOURS

The main ingredients of traditional Catalan dishes are typically Mediterranean: tomatoes, garlic, olive oil, aubergines (eggplant), courgettes (zucchini), peppers and herbs, which, when blended, form *samfaina*, a delicious sauce served with many dishes. Other principal sauces include *picada* (nuts, bread, parsley, garlic and saffron), *sofregit* (a simple sauce of onion, tomato and garlic lightly fried in olive oil) and *allioli* (a strong, garlicky mayonnaise).

For centuries *llom* (pork) has been the cornerstone of the Catalan diet. Little is wasted – even the *peus de porc* (pigs' trotters) are considered a delicacy. No bar would be complete without its haunch of *pernil* (cured ham), a popular *tapas* dish, and you often see a variety of sausages hanging from the rafters of restaurants and delicatessens. Lamb, chicken, duck, beef and game

also feature strongly, often prepared *a la brasa* (on an open charcoal grill) and served with a large serving of *allioli* (garlic mayonnaise).

MAR I MUNTANYA

In Catalan cuisine, meat is commonly combined with fruit, creating such mouth-watering dishes as *pollastre amb pera* (chicken with pears) and *conill amb prunes* (rabbit with prunes). However, it is the unique 'surf'n'turf' combinations that sea and mountain *(Mar i Muntanya)* produce which differentiates Catalan cuisine from the cookery of other Spanish regions. *Sépia amb mandonguilles* (cuttlefish with meatballs) and *mar i cel* ('sea and heaven' – made with sausages, rabbit, shrimp and fish) are especially tasty.

Near the coast, fish dishes reign supreme, ranging from simple grilled *sardinas* (sardines) and hearty *zarsuela* (seafood stew) to eye-catching

shellfish displays. Try *suquet de peix* (fish and potato soup) or the more unusual *broudegos* ('dog soup') made with fish, onions and orange juice, followed by speciality dishes *arròs negre* (rice cooked in black squid ink), *fideuá* (a local variant of paella, using vermicelli and noodles and not rice) or *bacallà* (salt cod), which comes *a la llauna* (with garlic, tomato and white wine), *esqueixada* (a salt cod and black olive salad), *amb samfaina* or *amb romesco* (a piquant sauce, made from a mixture of crushed nuts, tomatoes and spicy red pepper).

FINE WINES

A short distance south of Barcelona, the Penedès is the main Catalan wine region, producing red *(negre)*, white *(blanc)* and rosé *(rosat)* wines. Look for the reliable Torres, Masia Bach and René Barbier labels. Catalan *cava* (sparkling wine) also comes from the Penedès wineries, made by the *méthode champenoise*. Famous names include Freixenet and Codorníu, which can be sampled in the cava bars of Barcelona. To the north, the Alella and Empordà regions produce white wines, while Priorat produces excellent, heavy reds.

short break

If you have only a short time to visit Barcelona and would like to take home some unforgettable memories you can do something local and capture the real flavour of the city. The following suggestions will give you a wide range of sights and experiences that won't take very long, won't cost very much and will make your visit very special. If you only have time to choose just one of these, you will have found the true heart of the city.

- **Stroll along Las Ramblas** (➤ 50–51), pause for a coffee and enjoy the street performers.

- **Get into Gaudí,** especially Casa Milà (La Pedrera) (➤ 36–37), Park Güell (➤ 48–49) and the famous La Sagrada Família (➤ 52–53).

- **Follow in the footsteps** of Picasso and Dalí and wander at length through the maze of narrow streets in the Barri Gòtic (➤ 72–73, 86–88).

BAR
RESTAURANT

● **Enjoy the wide variety** of *tapas* (➤ 60–61) available in the local bars.

● **Join locals to dance** the *sardana*, the national dance of Catalonia (➤ 39).

● **Experience the tastes**, fragrances and colours of the Mediterranean at Mercat de la Boqueria (➤ 66).

● **Visit the Museu Picasso** (➤ 46–47).

● **Shop for Spanish fashion** and designer gifts in the smart Eixample district (➤ 142–145).

● **Watch FC Barça** play a home match (➤ 157).

● **Walk the waterfront** and sample the freshest of seafood.

Planning

Before you go

WHEN TO GO

JAN	FEB	MAR	APR	MAY	JUN	JUL	AUG	SEP	OCT	NOV	DEC
14°C	15°C	17°C	19°C	22°C	25°C	29°C	29°C	27°C	23°C	18°C	15°C
57°F	59°F	62°F	66°F	72°F	77°F	84°F	84°F	80°F	73°F	64°F	59°F

High season   Low season

Temperatures are the average daily maximum for each month.

The best time to visit Barcelona is May to June or September to October, when the weather is fine but not too hot, and there is a lot going on in the city. July and August see an exodus of locals and many museums, restaurants and shops either close or reduce their opening hours; day-trippers from coastal resorts crowd the city; and the weather can be hot and sticky, with some violent thunderstorms. On the upside, there are a handful of fiestas and festivals to keep you entertained. Winters are cool but seldom cold, and it rarely snows; when skies are blue and visibility perfect, January and February can be good months of the year.

WHAT YOU NEED

● Required
○ Suggested
▲ Not required

Some countries require a passport to remain valid for a minimum period (usually at least six months) beyond the date of entry – check before you travel.

	UK	Germany	USA	Canada	Australia	Ireland	Netherlands	Spain
Passport (or National Identity Card where applicable)	●	●	●	●	●	●	●	●
Visa (regulations can change – check before you travel)	▲	▲	▲	▲	▲	▲	▲	▲
Onward or Return Ticket	▲	▲	▲	▲	▲	▲	▲	▲
Health Inoculations (tetanus and polio)	▲	▲	▲	▲	▲	▲	▲	▲
Health Documentation (▶ 23, Health insurance)	●	●	●	●	●	●	●	●
Travel Insurance	○	○	○	○	○	○	○	○
Driving Licence (national)	●	●	●	●	●	●	●	●
Car Insurance Certificate	○	○	n/a	n/a	n/a	○	○	○
Car Registration Document	●	●	n/a	n/a	n/a	●	●	●

WEBSITES

City Council of Barcelona
www.bcn.es

Tourist Authority
www.barcelonaturisme.com

TOURIST OFFICES AT HOME

In the UK

Spanish Tourist Office
22–23 Manchester Square
London W1U 3PX
☎ (020) 7486 8077

In Germany

Kurfürstendamm 63, 5.OG
10707 Berlin
☎ (30) 8826543

In the US (New York)

Tourist Office of Spain
666 Fifth Avenue, 35th Floor
New York, NY 10103
☎ (212) 265-8822

In the US (Los Angeles)

Tourist Office of Spain
8383 Wilshire Blvd, Suite 960
Beverly Hills, CA 90211
☎ (323) 658-7188

HEALTH INSURANCE

Nationals of EU countries can obtain medical treatment at reduced cost with the relevant documentation (EHIC – European Health Insurance Card), although private medical insurance is still advised and is essential for all other visitors.

Dental treatment is not free of charge. A list of *dentistas* can be found in the yellow pages. Dental treatment should be covered by private medical insurance.

TIME DIFFERENCES

| GMT 12 noon | Barcelona 1 PM | Germany 1 PM | USA (NY) 7 AM | Netherlands 1 PM | Rest of Spain 1 PM |

Like the rest of Spain, Catalonia is one hour ahead of Greenwich Mean Time (GMT+1), except from late March to late October, when summer time (GMT+2) operates.

NATIONAL HOLIDAYS

1 Jan *New Year's Day*	11 Sep *Catalan National Day*	25 Dec *Christmas Day*
6 Jan *Three King's*	24 Sep *Our Lady of Mercy*	26 Dec *Sant Esteve*
19 Mar *Sant Josep*	12 Oct *Hispanitat*	
Mar/Apr *Easter*	1 Nov *All Saints' Day*	Most banks, businesses,
1 May *Labour Day*	6 Dec *Constitution Day*	museums and shops are
May/Jun *Whit Sunday*	8 Dec *Feast of the Immaculate Conception*	closed on these days.
24 Jun *St John*		
15 Aug *Assumption Day*		

WHAT'S ON WHEN

The venues and events listed here are liable to change from one year to the next and in the case of major festivals, there is often more than one venue. Dates also vary slightly from year to year.

January *Reis Mags* (6 Jan): the Three Kings arrive by boat the night before, then tour the city, showering the crowds with sweets.

February *Santa Eulàlia* (12–19 Feb): a series of cultural and musical events in honour of one of the city's patron saints.
Carnestoltes: one week of pre-Lenten carnival celebrations and costumed processions comes to an end on Ash Wednesday with the symbolic burial of a sardine.

March *Sant Medir de Gràcia* (3 Mar): procession of traditionally dressed horsemen from Gràcia who ride over Collserola to the Hermitage of Sant Medir (Saint of Broad Beans) for a bean-feast.

March/April *Setmana Santa:* religious services and celebrations for Easter Week include solemn processions by Spanish communities in outer Barcelona.

April *Sant Jordi* (23 Apr); Catalonia's most revered celebration when streets are thronging with rose and book sellers in honour of Saint George. Most museums and sights are free on this day.

June *Midsummer* (23–24 Jun) is a good excuse for partying and fireworks.
El Grec (end Jun–Aug); Barcelona's biggest arts festival with top names in music and theatre performing nightly.

July *Aplec de la Sardana*, Olot (second Sunday); the biggest *Sardana* dancing festival in Catalonia.

August *Festa Major de Gràcia* (3rd week of Aug): a popular festival of music, dancing and street celebrations in the Gràcia district (➤ 131).

September *Diada de Catalunya* (11 Sep): Catalonia's National Day does not mark a victory, but the taking of the city by Felipe V in 1714.
La Mercè (19–25 Sep): parades featuring giants, devils, dragons, big heads and fireworks, and free outdoor concerts.
Festa Major de la Barceloneta (last week of Sep): a lively district *feste*, with processions and dancing in the streets every night.

October *International Jazz Festival*: this huge festival draws many international names.

December *Christmas festivities* (end Nov–23 Dec): include a craft fair and trees outside the cathedral and a crib in Plaça Sant Jaume.

For more information about all the city's festivals while you are in Barcelona dial 010 (city hall information line) or visit the cultural information centre, La Palau de la Virreina, Las Ramblas 99.

Getting there

BY AIR
El Prat de Llobregat Airport

7km (4.3 miles) to city centre

 25 minutes

 20 minutes

15 minutes

Spain's national airline, Iberia, has scheduled flights to Barcelona's El Prat de Llobregat Airport from major Spanish and European cities. The city is served by over 30 international airlines and has direct flights to more than 80 international destinations. Non-stop flights are operated from New York by Iberia, in association with its partner in the Oneworld alliance, American Airlines. Most flights from North America involve a stop at Madrid or one of the other leading European airports, although Continental and Delta Airlines also fly nonstop to Barcelona from several US airports. From the UK and Ireland the lowest fares are often on no-frills airlines. These include easyJet, from Gatwick, Luton and Stansted and Ryan Air which flies from Stansted and Luton to Girona (80km/50 miles north of Barcelona) from where there is a bus to Barcelona. British Airways and its alliance partner, Iberia, fly from Gatwick, Heathrow, Birmingham and Manchester. British Midland (bmi) flies from Heathrow, and easyJet also flies from Liverpool. Iberia flies from Dublin, in association with its Oneworld partner Aer Lingus.There are no direct flights to Spain from Australia or New Zealand; connections via London, Frankfurt or Paris are the most common. Approximate flying times to Barcelona: London (1.5 hours), Liverpool (2 hours), New York (8 hours).

Flight prices tend to be highest in spring and summer (Easter to September). Check with airlines, travel agents, tour-operators and the internet for the current best deals.

BY RAIL
The main regional, national and international rail station is Sants-Estació. Comfortable, fast, express trains connect the city to Paris, Madrid and Valencia and other destinations in Europe.

BY ROAD

The AP7 highway connects the French border with Barcelona, a distance of only 166km (103 miles), though tolls are expensive. The AP2 connects the Spanish capital of Madrid with Barcelona, a distance of 660km (410 miles); most of the trip is also via toll roads. Well-paved and lit multi-lane toll roads are common all over Catalonia, and although free *carreteras nacionales* provide alternatives, they are generally less safe owing to poorer surfaces and lighting.

Getting around

PUBLIC TRANSPORT

Metro The metro is the easiest and fastest way of moving around the city. There are two different underground train systems, the Metro with its six lines identified by number and colour, and the FGC, an older service which is above ground in outer Barcelona. Both lines have been integrated into the same system (visit www.tmb.net for more information).

Buses Barcelona has an excellent bus network; pick up a free plan from any tourist office (or download from www.tmb.net). Timetables are also shown at individual bus stops. Buses run 6am–10pm. At night there is a *Nitbus* with routes centred on Plaça de Catalunya. Throughout the year the *Bus Turístic*, a hop-on, hop-off service, circuits the main city sights.

Trains The Spanish railway system, RENFE, runs trains from Barcelona to all the major cities in Spain and some outside. Many mainline trains stop at the underground stations at Passeig de Gràcia and Plaça de Catalunya. There are three main railway stations: Estació de Sants and Estació de França near Barceloneta, and Passeig de Gràcia in the Eixample.

Boat The best way to admire the port and coastline is from the sea. *Golondrinas* offer 35-minute harbour tours or 2-hour voyages to Port Olímpic (▶ 114–115). Barcelona is the biggest Mediterranean port, with regular passenger services to the Balearic islands and to Genoa and Rome.

Cable cars, funiculars and trams A cable car connects the lower city with Montjuïc castle and links with the funicular railway. The best way to reach Tibidabo is to take the FGC to the Peu de Funicular station, then the Funicular del Tibidabo to the Amusement Park at the top of the hill.

TAXIS

Pick up a black and yellow taxi at a taxi rank or hail one if it's displaying a green light and the sign *Lliure/Libre* (free). Fares are not unduly expensive but extra fees are charged for airport trips and for baggage, and at weekends and after 8:30pm. Prices are shown on a sticker inside.

DRIVING

- Drive on the right.
- Speed limits on motorways *(autopistas)*: 120kph/74mph; on main roads: 100kph/62mph; on minor roads: 90kph/55mph; in towns *(Poblaciones)*: 50kph/31mph.
- Seat belts must be worn at all times where fitted.
- Random breath-testing takes place. Never drive under the influence of alcohol.
- Fuel *(gasolina)* is available as: unleaded or *sin plomo* (90 octane), *gasoleo* or *gasoil* (diesel). *Super* (96 octane) is being phased out. Fuel stations are normally open 6am–10pm,though larger ones are open 24 hours. All take credit cards.

CAR RENTAL

The leading international car rental companies have offices at Barcelona airport and you can reserve a car in advance (essential in peak periods) either direct or through a travel agent. Local companies offer competitive rates and will usually deliver a car to the airport.

FARES AND CONCESSIONS

Travel cards (called *targetas*) come in options of 2 to 5 days or for 10 journeys (called a T-10) and are available from all Metro stations. They are valid for Metro, FGC, bus and some overland (RENFE) trains; transfers (on the same mode of transport) are allowed. With *targetas*, you generally end up paying half the price (or less, depending on the amount of travel you do) of a single journey (€1.30).

The Barcelona Card, available from tourist offices, offers savings on museums, sights and the hop-on, hop-off sightseeing *Bus Turístic*. Unlimited use of public transport is included. The cards are available in 2- or 5-day options (€17–€36).

Holders of an International Student Identity Card (ISIC) or Euro 26 card may obtain some concessions on travel and entrance fees. Most museums offer 50 per cent discount to students, and many are free on the first Sunday of each month. There are several IYHF youth hostels in the city, with accommodation in multi-bed dormitories. Expect to pay around €20–30 per person.

Barcelona is a popular destination for older travellers, especially during winter. Most museums and galleries offer a 50 per cent discount on entrance fees to older people.

Being there

TOURIST OFFICES

The main tourist office is situated beneath Plaça de Catalunya (and is well signposted). It provides a number of services including hotel reservations, currency exchange, walking tours and theatre and concert tickets.

There are branches of the city tourist office next to the city hall, at the Sants railway station and in front of the Columbus Monument (➤ 91).

There are also tourist information offices in the airport arrival halls, open daily 9–9.

● Turisme de Barcelona
Plaça de Catalunya 17
www.barcelonaturisme.com
☎ 93 368 97 30
🕔 Daily 9–9

● Plaça Sant Jaume I
🕔 Mon–Sat 10–8, Sun 10–2
Sants Railway Station (Estació de Sants)
🕔 Mon–Fri 8–8, Sat–Sun 8–2

● Turisme de Catalunya
Palau Robert
Passeig de Gràcia 107
www.gencat.net
☎ 93 285 38 34
🕔 Daily 9–9
In summer, information booths can be found at Sagrada Família and La Rambla. In the Barri Gòtic, you may also come across uniformed tourist officials, known as 'Red Jackets'.

MONEY

The euro (€) is the official currency of Spain. Banknotes are issued in denominations of €5, €10, €20, €50, €100, €200 and €500; coins are in denominations of 1, 2, 5, 10, 20 and 50 cents, and €1 and €2.

You can change travellers' cheques at banks and *caixes d'estalvis* (savings banks), at *oficines de canvi* (including late-night bureaux de change along Las Ramblas) and at stations and airports. Bureaux de change don't charge commission but apply less favourable rates.

Credit cards are widely accepted in shops, restaurants and hotels. All shops may require proof of identity such as ID card or passport (no copies). VISA, Mastercard and AMEX are the preferred cards, and they can be used to withdraw cash from widespread ATMs.

TIPS AND GRATUITIES

Yes ✓ No ✗		
Hotels (if service included)	✓	change
Restaurants	✓	5%
Cafés/bars	✓	change
Taxis	✓	change
Tour guides	✓	€1
Porters	✓	€1
Toilets	✗	

POSTAL AND INTERNET SERVICES

The main *Oficina Central* (post office) at Via Laietana 1 is open Mon–Sat 8:30am–9pm, and Sun 8–2. The Eixample post office at Carrer d'Aragó 282 is open Mon–Fri 8am–9pm and Sat 9–2pm. You can also buy stamps at any *estanc* (tobacconist).

WiFi internet access is becoming increasingly common in hotels and cafés. The cheapest internet access is found in *locutorios*, cheap call centres that are mainly clustered in El Raval neighbourhood. The biggest internet centre is easyEverything at Las Ramblas 31, open daily 8am–2:30am.

TELEPHONES

Increasingly public phones require a phonecard *(tarjeta)*. You can buy these from post offices, news-stands and *estancs* (tobacconists).

Calls from phones in bars and cafés are more expensive than those made from phone booths on the street. The best place to make international calls is from *locutorios* (phone centres), chiefly found in the Raval district. International cheap rates apply from 8pm to 8am and all weekend. If you are travelling with your mobile phone, prepaid call time and SIM cards are available, provided you own a GSM, dual or triband cellular phone.

International dialling codes
Dial 00 followed by
UK: 44
USA/Canada: 1
Irish Republic: 353
Australia: 61
France: 33
Germany: 49

Emergency telephone numbers
City police (Policía Municipal): 092
National police (Policía nacional): 091
Fire (Bomberos): 080
Ambulance (Ambuláncia) 061

EMBASSIES AND CONSULATES
UK ☎ 93 366 62 00
Germany ☎ 93 292 10 00
USA ☎ 93 280 22 27

Netherlands ☎ 93 363 54 20
France ☎ 93 270 30 00

HEALTH ADVICE
Sun advice The sunniest (and hottest) months are July and August, with an average of 11 hours of sun a day and daytime temperatures of 29°C (84°F). Whatever the month, avoid midday sun and use a strong sunblock.
Pharmacies Prescription and non-prescription drugs and medicines are available from *farmàcias* (pharmacies), distinguished by a large green cross. They are able to dispense many drugs that would be available only on prescription in some other countries.
Safe water Tap water is generally safe though it can be heavily chlorinated. Mineral water is cheap to buy and is sold as *con gas* (carbonated) and *sin gas* (still). Drink plenty of water during hot weather.

PERSONAL SAFETY

The *Guardia Urbana*, who control traffic, wear navy and pale blue uniforms. Disturbances are dealt with by the *Mossos d' Escquadra* (navy uniform with red braid), the local Catalan police force. More serious crime is dealt with by the *Policia Nacional,* who also take *denuncias* (statements) in the case of robbery. To help prevent crime:

- Do not carry more cash than you need.
- Do not leave valuables on the beach or poolside.
- Beware of pickpockets in crowded places.
- Avoid walking alone in dark alleys at night.
- Cars should be locked.

ELECTRICITY

The power supply is usually 220 volts but a few old buildings are still wired for 125 volts.

Sockets take two-round-pin-style plugs, so an adaptor is needed for most non-Continental appliances and a transformer for appliances operating on 110–120 volts.

OPENING HOURS

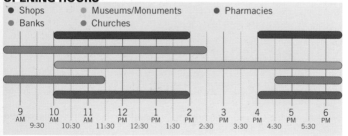

Large department stores and supermarkets may open outside these times, especially during the summer. Shops in the city centre don't close for lunch. Banks generally close on Saturdays, although main branches open in the morning 8:30–12:30. Outside banking hours, money-exchange facilities are available at the airport and Sants railway station. *Farmacias de Guardia* have extended opening hours. Some *barris* (districts) have their own feast days, when shops and offices may close.

LANGUAGE

In Barcelona, there are two official languages, Catalan and Spanish, both coming from Latin but both sounding quite different. Everybody can speak Spanish, although Catalan is also widely spoken. At most tourist sights you will always find someone who speaks English, and many restaurants have polyglot menus. However, it is advisable to try to learn at least some Catalan, since English is not widely spoken. Here is a basic vocabulary to help you with the most essential words and expressions.

yes	*si*	today	*avui*
no	*no*	tomorrow	*demà*
please	*per favor*	excuse me	*perdoni*
thank you	*gràcies*	how are you?	*com va?*
hello	*hola*	do you speak English?	*parla anglès?*
goodbye	*adéu*		
good morning	*bon dia*	I don't understand	*no ho enten*
good afternoon	*bona tarda*	how much?	*quant es?*
goodnight	*bona nit*	where is…?	*on és…?*
single room	*habitació senzilla*	bath	*bany*
double room	*habitació doble*	shower	*dutxa*
one night	*una nit*	toilet	*toaleta*
reservation	*reservas*	key	*clau*
room service	*servei d'habitació*	lift	*ascensor*
bank	*banc*	change	*camvi*
post office	*correos*	open	*obert*
credit card	*carta de crèdit*	closed	*tancat*
lunch	*dinar*	beer	*cervesa*
dinner	*sopar*	wine	*vi*
bill	*cuenta*	water	*aigua*
airport	*aeroport*	station	*estació*
train	*tren*	return ticket	*anar i tornar*
bus	*autobús*	non-smoking	*no fumar*

Best places to see

1 Casa Milà (La Pedrera)

www.lapedreraeducacio.org

This apartment block is Gaudí's last and most famous secular building. Its roof terrace is an iconic image of the city.

Built between 1906 and 1912, Casa Milà or La Pedrera shows this great Catalan architect at his most inventive. It also shows Gaudí's genius as a structural engineer, with seven storeys built entirely on columns and arches, supposedly without a single straight line or right-angled corner. Its most distinctive features are the rippling limestone façade, with its intricate ironwork, and the strangely shaped chimneys of the roof terrace. In fact, the large amount of limestone is what gave rise to the building's common name of La Pedrera (the quarry).

A visit to La Pedrera includes the Espai Gaudí, a gallery about the architect's work, and the Pis de Pedrera, an apartment decorated as it was when the building contained private residences. The rooftop, with its army of chimney stacks and incredible views is a highlight.

🚼 8F ✉ Carrer Provença 261–265
☎ 90 240 09 73
🕐 Mar–Oct daily 9–8; Nov–Feb daily 9–6
✋ Expensive
🚇 Diagonal ❓ Audio-guide available

2 Catedral

www.catedralbcn.org

Barcelona's great cathedral is not only one of the most celebrated examples of Catalan Gothic style, but also one of the finest cathedrals in Spain.

The cathedral is located at the heart of the Barri Gòtic (➤ 72–73, 86–88), on the remains of an early Christian basilica. Most of the building was erected between the late 13th century and the middle of the 15th century, although the heavily ornate main façade and octagonal dome were constructed at the beginning of the 20th century.

The impressive interior represents a harmonious blend of medieval and Renaissance styles, with a lofty triple nave, graceful arches, 29 side chapels and an intricately carved choir. Beneath the main altar is the crypt of Santa Eulàlia (the patron saint of Barcelona), which contains her tomb.

Near the main entrance is the Chapel of Christ of Lepanto (formerly the Chapter House), which is widely considered to be the finest example of

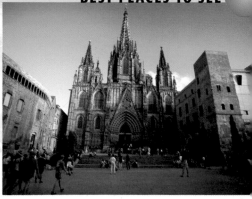

Gothic art in the cathedral. It contains the crucifix carried on board *La Real*, the flagship of Don Juan of Austria, during the famous Battle of Lepanto. The 14th-century cloister is the most beautiful part of the cathedral, its garden of magnolias, palms and fountains making a cool retreat. There is a small pond, with a flock of white geese, supposedly symbolizing Santa Eulàlia's virginal purity. A small museum just off the cloister shelters many of the cathedral's most precious treasures.

Despite its grandeur, the cathedral remains very much a people's church. The main entrance is on Plaça de la Seu and a side entrance along Carrer del Bisbe leads to the cloister. Worshippers outnumber tourists; on Sundays Barcelonans gather in Plaça de la Seu at noon to perform the *sardana*, Catalonia's stately national dance which symbolizes unity.

✚ *4c* ✉ Plaça de la Seu ☎ 93 310 71 95 ⏰ Mon–Fri 8–12:45, 5–7:30, Sat 8–12:45, 5–6; VIP: daily 1:30–4:30
👋 Free; VIP moderate 🚇 Jaume I 🚌 17, 19, 40, 45
❓ VIP entry also gives access to the roof and museum
Museum
⏰ Daily 10–12:45, 5–6:45 👋 Inexpensive
❓ Small gift shop

3 Fundació Joan Miró

www.bcn.fjmiro.es

This dazzling gallery pays homage to Joan Miró, one of Catalonia's greatest artists, famous for his childlike style and use of vibrant colours.

The Miró Foundation was set up by Joan Miró in 1971, and is devoted to the study of his works and to the promotion of contemporary art. The gallery – a modern building of white spaces, massive windows and skylights designed by Josep Lluís Sert – is itself a masterpiece and a perfect place in which to pursue the Foundation's aims. It contains some 240 Mirónian paintings, 175 sculptures, nine tapestries, his complete graphic works and more than 8,000 drawings, making it one of the world's most complete collections of this master.

Miró was born in Barcelona in 1893 and although, like many Catalan artists, he moved to Paris during the Civil War, his bold style of vigorous lines and intense primary colours owes much to the light and geography of Barcelona and Catalonia. In 1956 he moved to Mallorca, and remained on the island until his death in 1983.

Highlights of the gallery include some of Miró's earliest sketches, the tapestry *Tapis de la Fundació* and a set of black-and-white lithographs entitled *Barcelona Series* (1939–44) – an artistic appraisal of the war years. The roof terrace and gardens contain several striking sculptures.

The Foundation also presents temporary exhibitions of modern art, contemporary music recitals (➤ 154) and a special permanent collection called 'To Joan Miró', with works by Ernst, Tàpies, Calder and Matisse among others, a touching tribute to the person and his work.

✚ 16K ✉ Parc de Montjuïc ☎ 93 443 94 70 🕓 Oct–Jun Tue–Sat 10–7, Thu 10–9:30, Sun 10–2:30; Jul–Sep Tue–Sat 10–8, Thu 10–9:30, Sun 10–2:30 ✋ Moderate 🍴 Café (€€) 🚇 Espanya 🚌 50, 55

4 Montjuïc

Few can resist the charms of the city's local hill, with its museums, galleries, gardens and other attractions set in an oasis of natural calm.

Montjuïc, 213m (700ft) high, south of the city is the dominant feature of its skyline. Its history has been linked to the city's history since prehistoric times. The Romans later called it 'Jove's Mountain' but its present name is believed to be derived from 'Mountain of the Jews', after an early Jewish necropolis here. The castle, standing on the bluff, dates from the 16th to 18th centuries and houses the **Museu Militar,** exhibiting collections of military weaponry and uniforms.

Montjuïc was the venue for the International Expo in 1929. Today many of its buildings are filled with museums. The **Museu Arqueològic** and the **Museu Etnològic** typify the Expo's architecture, as does the Palau Nacional, home of the Museu Nacional d'Art de Catalunya (➤ 44–45).

Plaça d'Espanya marks the main entrance to the city's trade fair complex with Venetian towers, and an avenue leading to Plaça de la Font Màgica – 'Magic Fountain' – a spectacular sight. The road continues up past the **CaixaForum** modern art museum, Pavelló Mies van der Rohe (➤ 151) and the Poble Espanyol (➤ 152) to Fundació Joan Miró (➤ 40–41) and L'Anella Olímpica (➤ 148–149), a venue for the 1992 Olympic Games.

➕ 16K 🖐 Free 🍴 Cafés and restaurants (€–€€)
🚇 Espanya 🚌 50, 51, PM (Parc Monjuïc bus) 🚠 Montjuïc funicular from Paral.lel Metro station

Museums
☎ Museu Militar: 93 329 86 13. Museu Arqueològic: 93 424 65 77. Museu Etnològic: 93 424 68 07. CaixaForum: 93 476 86 00 🕐 Tue–Sun, times vary 🖐 Moderate

5 Museu Nacional d'Art de Catalunya (MNAC)

www.mnac.es

Dominating the northern flank of Montjuïc, this imposing neoclassical palace contains a treasure trove of Catalan art spanning several centuries.

The National Museum of Catalan Art is one of the best museums of medieval and Catalan art in the world. Housed in the extravagant National Exhibition building, built as the symbol of the 1929 World Exhibition (► 152), the museum boasts the world's most eminent Romanesque art collection. This includes stone sculptures, wood carvings, gold and silverwork, altar cloths, enamels and coins and a beautifully presented series of 11th- and 12th-century murals, carefully stripped from church walls throughout Catalonia and precisely reconstructed in apses, as if they were still in their original locations.

The idea for this collection originated in the early 20th century when the theft of national architectural treasures in Catalonia was at its height, instigating a church-led crusade to move

some of the region's most precious treasures to a safe location.

The museum's Gothic collection forms a striking contrast with more than 400 highly ornate retables and sculptures, including an extraordinary 15th-century Virgin in full flamenco dress. A somewhat frag-mented collection of Renaissance and baroque paintings embraces works by Tintoretto, El Greco and Zurbarán.

The modern art collection is devoted to Catalan art from the mid-19th century to around 1930. The collection starts with works by Maria Fortuny, the earliest of the *Modernistas* and the first Catalan artist to be known widely abroad, and friends Ramon Casas, whose work once hung on the walls of Els Quatre Gats (➤ 105), and Santiago Rusinyol. However, the highlight is the decorative arts collection: jewellery, textiles, stained glass and ironwork.

The building also contains the Museum of Drawings and Prints, the Numismatic Museum of Catalonia, and also houses the General Library of Art History.

🚻 15J 📧 Palau Nacional, Parc de Montjuïc ☎ 93 622 03 76 🕐 Tue–Sat 10–7, Sun and public hols 10–2.30 💷 Moderate; free first Sun of month 🍴 Café (€€) 🚇 Espanya 🚌 13, 37, 50, 55, 57, all buses to Plaça Espanya

Museu Picasso

www.museupicasso.bcn.es

This fascinating museum traces the career of the most acclaimed artist of modern times, from early childhood sketches to the major works of later years.

The Picasso Museum is the city's biggest tourist attraction. It contains one of the world's most important collections of Picasso's work and until 2003, when the impressive Museo Picasso Málaga opened in his birthplace, was the only one of significance in his native country.

Pablo Ruiz Picasso was born in Andalucía, but moved to Barcelona in 1895, aged 14. He was an exceptionally gifted artist and, by his first exhibition in 1900, was well known. In 1904 he moved to Paris, but remained in contact with Barcelona.

The museum contains work from his early years, notably a series of impressionistic landscapes and seascapes, a portrait of his aunt, Tía Pepa (1896), sketches and paintings of street scenes, *Sortida del Teatre* (1896) and La *Barceloneta* (1897), and the menu for *Els Quatre Gats* (Four Cats) café (➤ 105). Other works are from the Blue Period (1901–04), the Pink Period (1904–06), the Cubist (1907–20) and Neoclassical (1920–25) periods,

through to the mature works of later years. The
highlight of the collection is 'Las Meninas' – a
series of paintings inspired by the court painting of
Velázquez. There are 41 ceramic pieces donated in
1982 by his wife, Jacqueline, which demonstrate
Picasso's astonishing artistic development.

✚ 21K ✉ Carrer Montcada 15–23 ☎ 93 319 63 10
🕐 Tue–Sun 10–8 ✋ Moderate; free 11 Feb, 18 May and
24 Sep 🍴 Café-restaurant (€€) Ⓜ Jaume I 🚌 14, 17, 19,
40, 45

7 Park Güell

Deemed a failure in its day, Gaudí's eccentric hilltop park is now considered one of the city's treasures and a unique piece of landscape design.

The architectural work of Gaudí is inseparable from Barcelona, largely thanks to his relationship with the Güells, a family of industrialists who commissioned from him a number of works. For Park Güell, Don Eusebi Güell, Gaudí's main patron,

had grand ideas for a residential English-style garden city, with 60 houses set in formal gardens. Gaudí worked on the project from 1900 to 1914, but it proved an economic disaster: only three houses were completed, and the park became city property in 1923.

The park's main entrance is marked by two eccentric pavilions. A grand stairway, ornamented by a dragon fountain, leads to a massive cavernous space, originally intended as the marketplace. Its forest of pillars supports a rooftop plaza bordered by a row of curved benches, covered in multicoloured *trencadís* (broken ceramics).

Throughout the 20ha (50 acres) of Mediterranean parkland, there are sculptures, steps and paths raised on columns of 'dripping' stonework. Gaudí himself lived in one of the houses from 1906 to 1926. Built by his pupil Berenguer, it is now the Casa-Museu Gaudí and contains models, furniture, drawings and other memorabilia of the architect and his colleagues.

➕ 10C 📧 Main entrance: Carrer Olot ☎ 93 219 38 11
🕐 Daily 10–dusk 🍽 Free 🍴 Self-service bar
🚇 Lesseps or Vallcarca (and uphill walk with escalators)
🚌 24, 92, 116

8 Las Ramblas

Sooner or later, every visitor joins the locals swarming day and night down Las Ramblas, one of the most famous walkways in Spain.

The name Las Ramblas, derived from *ramla* (Arabic for 'torrent'), serves as a reminder that in earlier times, the street was a sandy gully that ran parallel to the medieval wall, and carried rainwater down to the sea. Today's magnificent 18th-century tree-lined walkway, running through the heart of the old city down to the port, is the pride of Barcelona. The central promenade is split into various distinctive sections strung head-to-tail, each with their own history and characteristics, from the flower stalls along Rambla de les Flors to the birdcages of Rambla dels Ocells. And it is said if you drink from the famous fountain in La Rambla de Canaletes you are sure to return to the city. The other parts of Las Ramblas are La Rambla dels Estudis, named after the university that was once here, La Rambla dels Caputxins, the section that's home to the

famous Liceu theatre, and La Rambla de Santa Mònica, the stretch nearest to the port.

Promenading Las Ramblas is never the same twice, changing with the seasons, by the day and by the hour. It's an experience eagerly shared by people from every walk of life – tourists, locals, bankers, Barça football fans, artists, beggars, street-performers, newspaper-sellers, pickpockets, nightclubbers, students, lovers and theatre crowds – all blending together with the noise of the traffic, the birdsong, the buskers (street musicians) and the scent of the flowers. Such is the significance to the city of this promenade *par excellence*, that two words – *ramblejar* (a verb meaning 'to walk down the Rambla') and *ramblista* (an adjective describing someone addicted to the act of *ramblejar)* – have been adopted in its honour.

✚ 19K or *1d* 🍴 Plenty (€–€€€) 🚇 Catalunya, Drassanes, Liceu 🚌 14, 38, 59, 91 ❓ Beware of pickpockets that may be in the area

9 La Sagrada Família

www.sagradafamilia.org

Big Ben, the Eiffel Tower...most cities have a distinctive monument. Barcelona has Gaudí's Sagrada Família, his, as yet unfinished, cathedral.

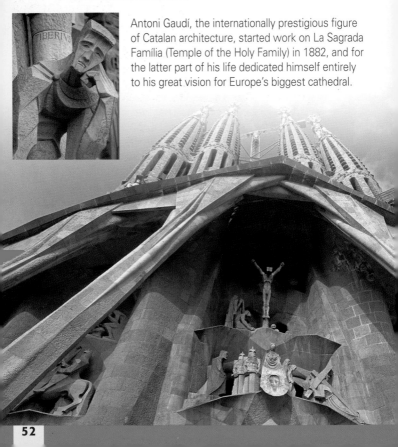

Antoni Gaudí, the internationally prestigious figure of Catalan architecture, started work on La Sagrada Família (Temple of the Holy Family) in 1882, and for the latter part of his life dedicated himself entirely to his great vision for Europe's biggest cathedral.

His dream was to include three façades representing the birth, death and resurrection of Christ, and eighteen mosaic-clad towers symbolizing the Twelve Apostles, the four Evangelists, the Virgin Mary and Christ. On his untimely death in 1926 (he was run over by a tram on the Gran Via), only the crypt, one of the towers, the majority of the east (Nativity) façade and the apse were completed. Ever since, the fate of the building has been the subject of often bitter debate.

With a further estimated 25 years of work (which would include the destruction of several buildings in Carrer Mallorca and Carrer Valencia), it seems that Gaudí's vision will eventually be realized. But even as it stands today, the cathedral is a world-wide symbol of Barcelona, one of the great architectural wonders of the world, and a must on every visitor's itinerary. A video about the history and construction of La Sagrada Família is included in the admission price.

✚ 23G ✉ Plaça Sagrada Família ☎ 93 207 30 31
🕒 Apr–Sep daily 9–8; Oct–Mar daily 9–6 💶 Expensive; additional charge for lift 🚇 Sagrada Família 🚌 19, 33, 34, 43, 44, 50, 51 ❓ Crypt museum, gift shop, lift and stairway to the towers

10 Santa Maria del Mar

This beautiful Gothic triumph was built to demonstrate Catalan supremacy in Mediterranean commerce.

The 14th-century church of Santa Maria del Mar (St Mary of the Sea) is at the heart of La Ribera (The Waterfront), the medieval city's maritime and trading district. This neighbourhood's link with the sea dates back to the 10th century, when a settlement grew up here along the seashore outside the city walls, around a chapel called Santa Maria de les Arenes (St Mary of the Sands). During the 13th century, the settlement grew and became known as Vilanova de Mar. Its identity was eventually firmly established with the transformation of the tiny chapel into the magnificent church of Santa Maria del Mar, built on what was then the seashore, as a show of maritime wealth and power. Indeed, the foundation stone commemorated the Catalan conquest of Sardinia.

The church was built between 1329 and 1384 and has a purity of style that makes it one of the finest examples of Barcelona's Gothic heritage. The plain exterior is characterized by predominantly horizontal lines and two octagonal, flat-roofed towers. Inside, the wide, soaring nave and high, narrow aisles, all supported by slim, octagonal

columns, provide a great sense of spaciousness. Sadly, the ornaments of the side chapels were lost when the city was besieged, once by Bourbon troops in 1714 and again during the Spanish Civil War. The resulting bareness of the interior, apart from the sculpture of a 15th-century ship that sits atop the altar, enables you to admire the church's striking simplicity without distraction.

➕ 21K ✉ Plaça de Santa Maria
☎ 93 310 23 90 🕒 Mon–Sat 9–1:30, 4:30–8, Sun 10–1:30, 4:30–8 ✋ Free
Ⓜ Barceloneta, Jaume I 🚌 14, 17, 19, 36, 39, 40, 45, 51, 57, 59, 64, 157

Best things to do

Great cafés

Cacao Sampaka

At the rear of a stylish chocolate 'boutique', this café serves hot chocolate on tap, as well as all sorts of cakes and pastries.

✉ Carrer Consell de Cent 292 ☎ 93 272 08 33 🚇 Passeig de Gràcia

Café Hotel Arts

Located inside the Picasso Museum (➤ 46) but open to all, this elegant café serves light snacks and lunches surrounded by the Gothic walls of the museum or outside in an interior courtyard.

✉ Carrer Montcada 15–23 ☎ 93 310 31 38 🚇 Jaume 1 ❓ No need to pay museum entrance

Café de l'Òpera

This original 19th-century café is one of Barcelona's favourites, and the best terrace-café along the Ramblas.

✉ La Rambla 74 ☎ 93 317 75 85 🚇 Liceu

Café Zurich

Popular bar and meeting place at the top of Las Ramblas. A great place for people-watching and soaking up the atmosphere.

✉ Plaça Catalunya 1 ☎ 93 317 91 53 🚇 Catalunya

Dulcinea

The most famous chocolate shop in town. Try *melindros* (sugar-topped sponge fingers) dipped in very thick hot chocolate.

✉ Carrer Petritxol 2 ☎ 93 302 68 24 🚇 Liceu

Granja M Viader

Atmospheric old *granja* tucked down a narrow pedestrian backstreet; you can expect to queue. Try a cup of hot chocolate and one of their delicious flaky pastries.

✉ Carrer Xuclà 4 ☎ 93 318 34 86 🕐 Closed Sun 🚇 Liceu

Laie Libreria Café

This quiet, elegant café is located on the first floor of one of the city's better bookshops, ensuring a good selection of newspapers and magazines to browse while you eat. It's great for a light lunch or coffee with a selection from their famous cake trolley.

✉ Carrer Pau Claris 85 ☎ 93 302 73 10 🚇 Passeig de Gràcia

Mesón del Café

Join locals at the bar for a coffee or hot chocolate while exploring the Barri Gòtic.

✉ Carrer de la Libreteria 16 ☎ 93 315 07 54 🕐 Closed Sun 🚇 Jaume I

Schilling

This spacious café and bar is an easy place in which to while away a hour or two sipping a coffee or a cocktail. Popular with a gay clientele and oozing understated elegance.

✚ Carrer Ferran 23 ☎ 93 317 67 87 🚇 Liceu

Tèxtil Cafè

Delicious light snacks in the courtyard of the medieval palace which houses the Museu Tèxtil.

✉ Carrer Montcada 12 ☎ 93 268 25 98 🕐 Closed Mon 🚇 Jaume I
❓ No need to pay museum entrance

Top *tapas* bars

Bar del Pi
Simple but popular, despite its small *tapas* selection, in one of Barcelona's most atmospheric squares.
✉ Plaça Sant Josep Oriol 1 ☎ 93 302 21 23 🕓 Closed Mon, 2 weeks Jan and 2 weeks Aug Ⓜ Liceu

Bodega Sepúlveda
Boquerones (fresh anchovies) are the speciality at this genuine locals' bar.
✉ Carrer Sepúlveda 173 bis ☎ 93 454 70 94 🕓 Closed Sun and 3 weeks Aug Ⓜ Universitat

Cal Pep
The queues start forming at 8pm at this hole-in-the-wall joint, testament to the fact that Cal Pep's seafood *tapas* is simply the best in the city.
✉ Plaça de les Olles 8 ☎ 93 310 79 61 🕓 Closed Sun Ⓜ Barceloneta

Celta
A Galician bar near the port, known for its fried *rabas* (squid) and its *patatas bravas* (potàtoes in a spicy mayonnaise), serving Galician white wine in traditional white ceramic cups.
✉ Carrer Mercè 16 ☎ 93 315 00 06 🕓 Closed Sun Ⓜ Drassanes, Barceloneta

Cerveceria Catalana
This buzzing *tapas* bar is one the best, with mountains of fresh morsels and sizzling seafood. Take a seat at the bar – it's more fun!
✉ Carrer Mallorca 236 ☎ 93 216 03 68 Ⓜ Passeig de Gràcia

Euskal Etxea
Of the many bars in Barcelona selling *pintxos* (Basque-style *tapas*) this is one of the best. Get here are at 7pm as they sell out fast.
✉ Placeta Montcada 1–3 ☎ 93 310 21 85 🕓 Closed Sun Ⓜ Jaume I

La Plata
One of several *tascas* (traditional bars) on this narrow medieval street, specializing in whitebait and tomato and onion salads.
✉ Carrer Mercè 28 ☎ 93 315 10 09 🕓 Closed Sun 🚇 Barceloneta

Sagardi
A fashionable bar, popular with the young pre-dinner crowd, and those wishing to make a meal out of the large portions of *tapas*.
✉ Carrer Argenteria 62 ☎ 93 319 99 93 🚇 Jaume I

Taller de Tapas
Written menus and helpful staff take the headache out of *tapas* ordering. The quality is excellent and there are two branches.
✉ Carrer Argenteria 51 ☎ 93 268 85 59 🚇 Jaume 1
✉ Plaça Sant Josep Oriol 9 ☎ 93 301 80 20 🚇 Liceu

Vaso de Oro
Try the melt-in-your-mouth *solomillo,* beer made on the premises and superb *tapas* in what must be the narrowest bar in Barcelona.
✉ Carrer Balboa 6 ☎ 93 319 30 98 🚇 Barceloneta

Excellent restaurants

Agut d'Avignon
Hidden up an alleyway off Calle d'Avinyó at the heart of the Barri Gòtic, with classic Catalan cuisine that attracts politicians, artists and even the King of Spain.
✉ Carrer Trinitat 3 ☎ 93 302 60 34 🚇 Jaume I

Alkimia
Superb restaurant with chef Jordi Vila at the helm, serving wonderfully innovative dishes in a sleek dining room.
✉ Carrer Industria 79 ☎ 93 207 61 15 🕓 Closed Sat and Sun 🚇 Sagrada Família

Can Majó
The city's top seafood restaurant. The *suquet de peix* (mixed fish casserole), *arroz negre* (black rice) with *bacalao* (salt cod) or lobster, and *centollos* (crabs from the north coast) are delicious.
✉ Carrer Almirall Aixada 23 ☎ 93 221 54 55 🕓 Closed Sun dinner and Mon 🚇 Barceloneta

Casa Calvet
Gaudí's first apartment building in Barcelona is now a sumptuous restaurant offering sophisticated French and Catalan cuisine.
✉ Carrer Casp 48 ☎ 93 412 40 12 🕓 Closed Sun 🚇 Urquinaona

Cinc Sentits
A minimalist restaurant serving New Catalan Cuisine. Try the tasting menu with wine pairing for the full experience.
✉ Carrer Aribau 58 ☎ 93 323 94 91 🕓 Closed Mon dinner and Sun 🚇 Passeig de Gràcia

La Dama
The French cuisine of this Michelin star-rated restaurant rivals that of the top restaurants of Paris. A bonus is the *Modernista* setting.
✉ Avinguda Diagonal 423 ☎ 93 202 06 86 🚇 Diagonal

El Lobito

For fish aficionados, this is the ultimate experience. There is no menu: just take a seat and mountains of the freshest seafood in all its forms will be brought to your table.

✉ Carrer Ginebra 9 ☎ 93 319 91 64 🕔 Closed Sun and Mon 🚇 Barceloneta

Set Portes

One of Barcelona's most historic restaurants, serving excellent Catalan cuisine in traditional surroundings.

✉ Passeig de Isabel II 14 ☎ 93 319 30 33 🚇 Barceloneta

Tapioles 53

This intimate space serves European and Asian dishes. Ingredients are sourced daily from local markets. Reservations are essential.

✉ Carrer Tapioles 53 ☎ 93 329 22 38 🕔 Dinner only; closed Sun and Mon 🚇 Paral.lel

Torre de Alta Mar

Classy cuisine served in a glass-enclosed dining room perched on top of a cable-car tower. Needless to say, the views are fabulous.

✉ Passeig de Joan de Borbó 88 ☎ 93 221 00 07 🕔 Closed Sun 🚇 Barceloneta

Stunning views

Casa Milà (La Pedrera) rooftop terrace (➤ 36–37)

Monument a Colom (➤ 91)

Park Güell (➤ 48–49)

Museu Nacional d'Art de Catalunya (MNAC) terrace (▶ 44–45)

La Sagrada Família (▶ 52–53)

Torre de Collserola (▶ 159)

Markets

Barceloneta

This imaginative makeover of a 19th-century market is a landmark.
Excellent bars and restaurants jostle with traditional fish stalls.
✉ Plaça Font 1 🕐 Mon, Sat 7–3, Tue–Thu 7–3, 5–8:30 🚇 Barceloneta

La Boqueria

Superb 19th-century market hall at the heart of Las Ramblas. Top
quality fresh produce including fish, fruit, vegetables and herbs.
🕐 Mon–Sat 8–8 🚇 Liceu

Els Encants

Flea market with second-hand toys, clothes and accessories,
kitchen goods and other reminders of the past.
✉ Plaça de les Glòries 🕐 Mon, Wed, Fri, Sat 9–3 🚇 Glòries, Encants

Fira de Santa Lucia

Located in front of the cathedral (➤ 38) the Christmas market is the biggest event during *Nadal*. Christmas trees and decorations, Nativity figures, plus artisan crafts and gifts in hundreds of stalls.

✉ Plaça de la Seu ⏰ End Nov–23 Dec 10–8 Ⓜ Jaume 1, Liceu

Plaça del Pi

Outdoor market selling home-made honey, herbs and cheeses.

⏰ First and third Fri, Sat and Sun of month 10–10 Ⓜ Liceu

Plaça Reial

Browse among the stands displaying coins and stamps every Sunday. Also stalls with general items of interest for sale.

⏰ Sun 9–2:30 Ⓜ Liceu, Drassanes

Plaça Sant Josep Oriol

Art market in one of the Barri Gòtic's picturesque squares.

⏰ Sat 11–10, Sun 10–3 Ⓜ Liceu

Raval craft and hippy market

Funky, handmade clothes, crafts and accessories, plus Moroccan tea stalls make up this small but eclectic market.

✉ Rambla del Raval (northern end) ⏰ Weekends only Ⓜ Sant Antoni, Liceu

Santa Caterina

A modern, new market, held in the Barri Gòtic, with striking architecture (including 109 arches) featuring a variety of traditional stalls, restaurants and bars.

✉ Francesc Cambó 16 ⏰ Thu, Fri 7:30am–8:30pm, Tue, Wed, Sat 7:30–3:30, Mon 7:30–2 Ⓜ Jaume 1

Places to take the children

L'Aquàrium
Aquatic life on display and a tunnel through the shark tank.
www.aquariumbcn.com
✉ Moll d'Espanya, Port Vell ☎ 93 221 74 74 🕓 Jul–Aug daily 9:30am–11pm; Sep–Jun daily 9:30–9:30 👋 Expensive 🚇 Barceloneta, Drassanes

Beaches
The city has 4km (2.5 miles) of clean, sandy beaches with playgrounds, palm-lined promenades and shower facilities.
✉ Platja de Barceloneta, Nova Icària, Bogatell and La Nova Mar Bella
🚇 Ciutadella, Selva de Mar, Poble Nou, Barceloneta

CosmoCaixa
At this superb science museum children can feel an earthquake and visit an Amazon-style rainforest.
✉ Carrer Teodor Roviralta 55 ☎ 93 212 60 50 🕓 Tue–Sun 10–8
👋 Inexpensive 🚇 Avinguda Tibidabo, then Tramvia Blau or 10-minute walk

IMAX Cinema
Nature and action films on IMAX's giant 3-D screen (➤ 100).
✉ Moll d'Espanya, Port Vell ☎ 93 225 11 11 👋 Expensive 🚇 Barceloneta, Drassanes

Museu de la Cera
Pinocchio, Superman and other heroes at the Waxwork Museum.
✉ Passeig de la Banca 7 ☎ 93 317 26 49 🕓 Jul–Sep daily 10–10; Oct–Jun Mon–Fri 10–1:30, 4–7:30, Sat–Sun 11–2, 4:30–8:30 👋 Moderate
🚇 Drassanes

Museu del Futbol Club Barcelona
A must for all children who are keen on football (➤ 157).
www.fcbarcelona.com
✉ Nou Camp – Gate 7 or 9 (Carrer Arístides Maillol) ☎ 93 496 36 00
🕓 Mon–Sat 10–8, Sun 10–2 👋 Moderate 🍴 Café

Museu de la Xocolata

Hands-on museum about the history of chocolate and chocolate making. A café serving cocoa-based delights rounds off the visit.

✉ Carrer Comerç 36 ☎ 93 268 78 78 🕐 Mon–Sat 10–7, Sun 10–3 ✋ Moderate 🚇 Arc de Triomf, Jaume 1

Parc d'Atraccions del Tibidabo

An authentic, old-fashioned fairground atmosphere with carousels, bumper cars, a hall of mirrors and an open ferris wheel.

✉ Plaça Tibidabo 3–4 ☎ 93 211 79 42 🕐 Jul–Aug Wed–Sat noon–11; call ahead for other times ✋ Expensive 🚇 FGC Tibidabo, then Tramvia Blau, then Funicular del Tibidabo

Parc Zoològic

Spain's top zoo has a section for the under-fives, where children can stroke farm animals and pets, and a dolphinarium.

www.zoobarcelona.com

✉ Parc de la Ciutadella ☎ 93 225 67 80 🕐 Jun–Sep 10–7; Mar–May, Oct 10–6; Nov–Feb 10–5 ✋ Expensive 🚇 Barceloneta

Poble Espanyol

This 'model village' contains examples of Spain's regional architecture, from Castilian castles to pretty whitewashed houses.

✉ Avinguda Marqués de Comillas s/n ☎ 93 508 63 00 🕐 Mon 9am–8pm, Tue–Thu 9am–2am, Fri 9am–4am, Sat 9am–5am, Sun 9am–midnight ✋ Moderate 🚇 Espanya

Activities

Walking: take a stroll down Las Ramblas (➤ 50–51), the vibrant heart of the city.

Rickshaws: a fun way to get around, they can be hailed on the street around the old city and Port Vell.
www.trixi.com
🕐 Daily 11–8

Bus tours: a circuit around the city on the Bus Turístic with 25 stops at key points of interest is a good way to see the sights.
✉ Plaça de Catalunya (or any of its 25 stops) 🕐 First bus leaves Plaça de Catalunya at 9am 🚇 Catalunya

Cycling: this has taken off in a big way in Barcelona, prompted by better cycle lanes and Bicing, the city's bike-share service (for residents only). Inexpensive bicycle hire for tourists is available at the tourist office. Fat Tire Bike Tours offers guided tours.
www.fattirebiketoursbarcelona.com
✉ Escudellers 48 ☎ 93 301 36 12 ✋ Moderate

***Golondrinas* (pleasure boats):** take a pleasure boat tour of the old harbour or the Port Olímpic. The most fun is a trip out to the breakwater on one of the old wooden 'swallow boats', which have been operating since 1888 (➤ 100).
✉ Moll de les Drassanes Plaça Portal de la Pau ☎ 93 442 31 06

Jogging and running: start at Barceloneta beach and continue to the Hotel Arts (about 2km/1 mile) or on to the Forum complex in Poble Nou (about 5km/3 miles).
Ⓜ Barceloneta, Ciutadella-Vila Olímpica, El Maresme-Forúm

Swimming: Piscines Bernat Picornell. This attractive swimming pool in Montjuïc is part of the Anella Olímpica, or Olympic complex.
✉ Avinguda de l'Estadi ☎ 93 423 40 41 Ⓜ Paral.lel, then funicular to Montjuïc 🚌 55

Ice skating: FC Barcelona Pista de Gel. Home to Barcelona's only professional ice-hockey team. Gloves must be worn and are on sale at the venue.
✉ Nou Camp, entrance 7 or 9, Avinguda de Joan XXIII ☎ 93 496 36 00 ✋ Moderate Ⓜ Maria Cristina, Collblanc

Tennis: Centre Municipal Tennis Vall d'Hebron is where tennis matches of the 1992 Olympic Games were played.
✉ Passeig Vall d'Hebron 178–196 ☎ 93 427 65 00 🚌 17, 27, 60

a walk

through the Barri Gòtic

Leave tiny Plaça Nova on the right-hand side of the cathedral via the Portal del Bisbe (part of the Roman wall) into Carrer del Bisbe. Turn first left into Carrer de Santa Llúcia.

Note the tiny chapel of Santa Llúcia to your right, and the Gothic Archdeacon's House (Casa de l'Ardiaca) to your left. Just beyond is the main entrance to the Catedral (➤ 38–39).

From Plaça de la Seu, follow Carrer dels Comtes to the left of the cathedral, past Museu Frederic Marès (➤ 93). Turn left into Baixada de Santa Clara to Plaça del Rei (➤ 97). Return to the cathedral and skirt round its buttresses past the 14th-century Canon's House (Casa del Cánonges).

Stone plaques on the façade portray towers supported by winged goats with lions' feet, heraldic symbols of medieval Barcelona.

Turn sharp left, then left again onto Carrer del Bisbe, go under a bridge and into Plaça Sant Jaume (➤ 99). Take Carrer de la Ciutat, then first left to Plaça Sant Just.

Església dels Sants Just i Pastor is reputedly Barcelona's oldest church.

Leave the square along Carrer del Lledó. Turn right and walk to tiny Plaça Traginer and the most intact part of the old Roman walls.

Constructed between AD 270 and 310, Barcelona's Roman walls were outgrown by the 11th century.

For more Roman vestiges, turn right into Carrer Correu Vell and right again into Carrer Regomir.

At No 3 is Pati Llimona, where the remains of a Roman dwelling are visible through a glass floor.

Continue walking along Carrer Regomir to Plaça Nova.

Distance 2km (1.25 miles)
Time 1 hour (excluding visits)
Start/end point Plaça Nova ✚ 3b
Ⓜ Catalunya, Urquinaona
Coffee break Mesón del Café (€)
✉ Carrer Llibreteria 16, just off Plaça Sant Jaume I ☎ 93 315 07 54

Parks and gardens

Jardí Botànic

A contemporary landscape garden divided into eight different zones displaying plants from Australia to the Balearic Islands.
www.jardibotanic.bcn.es

➕ 15J ✉ Carrer Doctor Fonti Quer 2 ☎ 93 426 49 35 🕐 Jun–Aug daily 10–8; Apr, May, Sep daily 10–7; Feb, Mar, Oct daily 10–6; Nov–Jan daily 10–5 ✋ Moderate 🍴 Snack bar 🚌 50, 51, PM (Parc Montjuïc) bus

Montjuïc

The city's finest and largest park, rising over the harbour, offers both exotic gardens and fine museums (➤ 42–43).

➕ 16K 🍴 Snack bar 🚇 Espanya 🚌 50, 51, PM (Parc Montjuïc) bus
🚋 Montjuïc funicular from Paral.lel

Palau Reial de Pedralbes gardens

The landscaped park surrounding the Royal Palace of Pedralbes is perfect for a picnic (➤ 158–159).

➕ 2C ✉ Avinguda de la Diagonal 686 🕐 Park: daily 10–dusk ✋ Park: free
🚇 Palau Reial 🚌 7, 33, 67, 68, 74, 75

Parc de la Ciutadella

A great place for a walk, a picnic or boating on the lake (➤ 120).

➕ 22K ✉ Main entrance: Passeig Picasso 🕐 Daily 10–dusk 🍴 Snack bar
🚇 Arc de Triomf, Barceloneta, Jaume I

Parc de la Creueta del Coll

An old stone quarry makes for Barcelona's most unusual park, with an enormous bronze sculpture suspended over a rock-lined pool.

➕ 10B ✉ Carrer Cardedeu s/n 🕐 10–dusk 🍴 Snack bar 🚌 27, 28, 92

Parc de l'Espanya Industrial

Located on the site of an old textile factory, the park has some surreal sculptures and a small boating lake (➤ 150).

➕ 15G ✉ Carrer de Muntadas 🍴 Snack bar 🚇 Sants-Estació

Parc de l'Estació del Nord

Behind the main bus station this modern park borders on land art, with evocative sculptures by US artist Beverly Pepper.

➕ 22J ✉ Carrer Napoles 1 🕐 Open all the time 🚇 Arc de Triomf

Parc de Joan Miró (Parc de l'Escoraxdor)

A popular park with pergolas and shady palm trees. Its most famous feature is the sculpture *Dona i Ocell* (Woman and Bird) by Miró (➤ 150–151).

➕ 16G ✉ Carrer de Tarragona 🍴 Snack bar 🚇 Tarragona, Espanya

Parc del Laberint

An extensive garden with fountains, sculptures and a beautiful maze at its heart, from which the park takes its name. Situated on the wooded slopes of Vall d'Hebron.

➕ 10A (off map) ✉ Carrer Germans Desvalls, Vall d'Hebron ☎ 93 428 25 00 🕐 Daily 10 until dark, ticket office closes one hour before closing time ✋ Inexpensive; free Wed and Sun 🍴 Snack bar 🚇 Mundet 🚌 10, 27, 60, 73, 76, 85

Park Güell

Gaudí's fairytale park overlooking the city (➤ 48–49).

➕ 10C ✉ Main entrance: Carrer Olot ☎ 93 219 38 11 🕐 Daily 10–dusk ✋ Free 🍴 Snack bar 🚇 Lesseps or Vallcarca (and uphill walk) 🚌 24, 28

Modernista and modern architecture

Casa Batlló (➤ 134–135)

Casa Milà (La Pedrera) (➤ 36–37)

Casa Lleó-Morera (➤ 135)

Fundació Antoni Tàpies (➤ 130)

Hospital de la Santa Creu i Sant Pau (➤ 132–133)

Palau Güell (➤ 95)

Palau de la Música Catalana (➤ 118–119)

Park Güell (➤ 48–49)

Pavelló Mies van der Rohe (➤ 151)

La Sagrada Família (➤ 52–53)

Street art

Peix (Fish)
Designed by American architect Frank Gehry, the giant bronze fish by the beach is the city's maritime symbol (▶ 115).
✉ Hotel Arts, Passeig Marítim, Port Olímpica

Cap de Barcelona (Barcelona Head)
A giant mosaic sculpture by Roy Lichtenstein at the eastern end of the waterfront promenade just in front of the main post office.
✉ Plaça Antonio López

Gambrinus
A giant rooftop fibreglass lobster by Xavier Mariscal.
✉ Moll de la Fusta, Passeig de Colom

Dona i Ocell (Woman and Bird)
A startling sculpture covered in multicoloured ceramic fragments, in Parc de Joan Miró (▶ 151).
✉ Carrer de Tarragona

Nüvol i Cadira (Cloud and Chair)
An eye-catching tangle of wire and tubes on the roof of Fundació Antoni Tàpies (▶ 130).
✉ Carrer d'Aragó 255

El Gato (The Cat)
This voluptous bronze cat figure is by Columbian artist Fernando Botero.
✉ Rambla del Raval

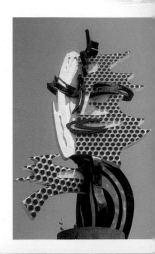

Estil Ferit (Homage to Barceloneta)
German artist Rebecca Horn's stacked steel cubes are homage to the old *chiringuitos* (beach bars) of Barceloneta beach.
✉ Platja de la Barceloneta

Els Gegants, La Senyera i Les Nens

This mural on the wall of the city's architecture school was designed by Picasso and features Catalan folkloric figures.

✉ Plaça Nova 1

La Senyoreta del Paraigua (The Lady with the Umbrella)

This elegant belle époque sculpture is the work of Josep Foresteré, designer of the park where it is located.

✉ Parc de la Ciutadella (inside zoo)

Barcino

Outside the main cathedral, Joan Brossa's giant bronze letters are homage to the old Roman city.

✉ Plaça de la Seu

Best shopping

Caleum

For a great gift to take home, this lovely shop sells cakes, jams, honey and other delights produced in convents and monasteries all over Spain. There is a café on site to try before you buy.

✉ Carrer Palla 8 ☎ 93 302 69 93 Ⓜ Liceu

Centre Català d'Artesania

The impressive centre of Catalan handicrafts contains some of the finest ceramics, jewellery, textiles, sculptures and glassware of the region.

✉ Passeig de Gràcia 55 ☎ 93 467 46 60 Ⓜ Passeig de Gràcia

Custo Barcelona

Another successful export, Custo's loud and funky T-shirts have now reached celebrity status. They have recently added eclectic coats and skirts to their range.

✉ Plaça de les Olles 7 (also Las Ramblas 109) ☎ 93 268 78 93; www.custo-barcelona.com Ⓜ Jaume I

FNAC

A book megastore inside El Triangle shopping mall. Two floors of books, DVDs, CDs, computers, PlayStations, computer games and magazines from all over the world.

✉ El Triangle, Plaça de Catalunya ☎ 93 344 18 00
🕐 Mon–Sat 10–10 Ⓜ Catalunya

Loewe

One of the most celebrated leather-goods companies in the world, located in Domènech i Montaner's *Modernista* Lleó-Morera building.

✉ Passeig de Gràcia 35 ☎ 93 216 04 00 Ⓜ Passeig de Gràcia

La Manual Alpargatera

This shop has been making traditional Spanish espadrilles, with esparto soles, by hand since 1910. Their footwear has been worn by celebrities including Michael Douglas and Jack Nicholson.

✉ Carrer Avinyó 7 ☎ 93 301 01 72 🚇 Jaume I, Liceu

Museu Picasso

One of Barcelona's many notable museum shops reflecting the city's connections with this major 20th-century artist.

✉ Carrer Montcada 15 ☎ 93 319 63 10 🚇 Jaume I

Vinçon

This design 'department store' is Barcelona's answer to the British designer Terance Conran. Trendy yet practical household articles at accessible prices.

✉ Passeig de Gràcia 96 ☎ 93 215 60 50 🚇 Passeig de Gràcia

Xocoa

The offspring of this dynasty of chocolate-makers has created a brilliant concept of designer-packaged chocolate bars and bon-bons in unusual flavours.

✉ Carrer Petrixol 11–13 (and all over the city) ☎ 93 301 1197; www.xocoa-bcn.com 🚇 Liceu

Zara

The Spanish fashion label that conquered the world has a bigger range at better prices on its home turf. Larger stores include Zara Home (textiles and homeware), which is exclusive to Spain.

✉ Passeig de Gràcia 16 (and all over the city) ☎ 93 318 76 75; www.zara.com 🚇 Passeig de Gràcia

Exploring

Ever since it was founded more than 2,000 years ago, Barcelona has been striving to become a great metropolis. To its inhabitants, it is not Spain's second city but the capital of Catalonia; not a Spanish metropolis but a European one, and the Spanish leader in both *haute couture* and *haute cuisine*. The best time to see Barcelona in its true colours is after FC Barça wins an important match, and the streets erupt to the sound of car horns and popping champagne corks.

Visitors to Barcelona, on the other hand, are entranced by the Mediterranean atmosphere of the city, the richness of its art and architectural treasures both ancient and modern, the proud but not narrowly nationalistic character of the people, the strong tradition of theatre and music and the exuberant nightlife. In this dynamic and passionate city, it is easy to live life to the fullest, both day and night.

Las Ramblas and around

Las Ramblas, one long tree-lined thoroughfare divided into five distinct sections, stretches from Plaça de Catalunya, Barcelona's main square, towards the waterfront. It is the place to sit, to watch street entertainers and, in time, be drawn into the ceaseless flow of pedestrians.

To the left of Las Ramblas is the Barri Gòtic (Gothic Quarter), a maze of dark narrow streets around the cathedral, medieval palaces and churches. Beyond is Port Vell (Old Port), the colourful harbourside, with a marvellous state-of-the-art aquarium, and the Maremagnum, a huge covered entertainment and shopping complex. Antoni Gaudí's magnificent palace, Palau Güell, off the end of the Ramblas in the direction of the port, is set in the lower side of El Raval – a run-down mix of medieval streets, gloomy alleyways and dead-ends. By contrast, the upper part of El Raval is now dominated by the Museu d'Art Contemporàni (MACBA), Barcelona's contemporary art museum set amid stylish restaurants and art galleries galore.

BARRI GÒTIC

The tightly packed maze of narrow streets and alleyways of Barcelona's Ciutat Vella (Old City), bordered by Las Ramblas, the Ciutadella Park, Plaça Catalunya and the sea, was once enclosed by medieval city walls and, until the massive building boom of the Eixample (➤ 129), 150 years ago, comprised the entire city.

At its heart is the Barri Gòtic (Gothic Quarter), one of several clearly identifiable *barris* or districts which make up the Old City. Its roots can be traced back to 15BC, when Roman soldiers established a small settlement called Barcino on a slight hill here called Mons Taber. This remarkable cluster of dark, twisting streets, quiet patios, sun-splashed squares and grand Gothic buildings was built inside the Roman fortifications at a time when Barcelona, along with Genoa and Venice, was one of the three most important merchant cities in the Mediterranean and possessed untold riches. Its crowning glory, the Catedral (➤ 38–39), is surrounded by former residences of the counts of Barcelona and the Kings of Catalonia and Aragón. To the northwest lies Carrer Portaferrissa, the principal shopping street, with sophisticated boutiques and shopping arcades. To the south lies the spacious Plaça Sant Jaume (➤ 99) and a cobweb of narrow streets and interconnecting squares, including Plaça Sant Felip Neri, with its fine baroque church, Plaça del Pi, with its market of local produce (➤ 67), and leafy Plaça Sant Josep Oriol, the 'Montmartre of Barcelona', where local artists display their works at weekends and buskers entertain the café

crowds. Just off the square, the narrow streets bounded by Carrer Banys Nous, Call and Bisbe once housed a rich Jewish ghetto called *El Call*, but now the area is better known for its antiques shops.

As the city grew more prosperous in the early Middle Ages, new *barris* developed around the Roman perimeter, including La Mercè to the south and La Ribera to the east. La Ribera is the old city's most fashionable district, with a plethora of cutting-edge cafés and boutiques, and dominated by the majestic Santa Maria del Mar church (➤ 54–55). The area south of Carrer de Ferran – La Mercè – is focused around the elegant, arcaded Plaça Reial (➤ 98) and the Church of La Mercè, Barcelona's patron Virgin.

✚ 20K or *3c*

CATEDRAL
Best places to see, ➤ 38–39.

DRASSANES REIALS AND MUSEU MARÍTIM
The Museu Marítim (Maritime Museum) is in the magnificent Drassanes Reials (Royal Shipyards), a splendid example of Gothic civil architecture. Since the 13th century, these yards have been dedicated to the construction of ships for the Crowns of Catalonia and Aragon.

Today, their vast cathedral-like, stone-vaulted halls contain maps, charts, paintings, pleasure craft and a huge range of other seafaring memorabilia chronicling the remarkable maritime history of Barcelona. The most impressive exhibit is a 60m (66yds) replica of *La Real*, flagship of Don Juan of Austria, which forms part of an exciting 45-minute spectacle – 'The Great Sea Adventure'. Through headphones, visual and acoustic effects, visitors can experience life as a galley slave, encounter a Caribbean storm, join emigrants bound for the New World, and explore the seabed on board *Ictineo*, claimed to be the world's first submarine and built by Catalan inventor Narcís Monturiol.

www.museumaritimbarcelona.org

✠ 19L ✉ Avinguda de les Drassanes s/n ☎ 93 342 99 29 ⊕ Daily 10–8
✋ Expensive 🍴 Café-restaurant (€€) Ⓜ Drassanes 🚌 14, 18, 36, 38, 57, 59, 64, 91 ❓ Library, bookshop, gift shop

MERCAT DE LA BOQUERIA

Of more than 40 food markets in Barcelona, La Boqueria is the best and the busiest – always bustling with local shoppers, restaurateurs, gourmands and tourists. Its cavernous market hall (best entered through an imposing wrought-iron entranceway halfway up Las Ramblas) was built in the 1830s to house the food stalls that cluttered Las Ramblas and surrounding streets.

Inside is a riot of noise, aromas and colours, with a myriad of stalls offering all the specialities of the Mediterranean and the Catalonian hinterland – mouth-watering displays of fruit and vegetables, a glistening array of exotic fish, endless strings of sausages, haunches of ham and sweetly scented bunches of herbs.

✚ 19J or *1b* ✉ Rambla 91 ☎ 93 318 25 84
🕐 Mon–Sat 8–8. Closed public hols
🍴 Snack bars (€) 🚇 Liceu

MONUMENT A COLOM

This vast monument, commemorating the return of Christopher Columbus to Barcelona in 1493 from his first trip to the Americas, stands outside the naval headquarters of Catalonia, at the seaward end of the Ramblas. It was designed by Gaietà Buigas for the Universal Exposition of 1888, with Columbus standing at the top of a column 50m (164ft) high, pointing out to sea – towards Italy! Take the lift to the top for breathtaking bird's-eye views of the harbourfront.

✚ 19L or *1f* ✉ Plaça Portal de la Pau ☎ 93 302 52 24 ⏰ Daily 9–8:30
✋ Inexpensive 🚇 Drassanes

MUSEU D'ART CONTEMPORANI DE BARCELONA (MACBA)

The Barcelona Museum of Contemporary Art (MACBA), which celebrated its 10th anniversary in 2005, focuses on the art movements of the second half of the 20th century.

The building, itself a work of art, was designed by the American architect Richard Meier. It has been the subject of much controversy but is increasingly being included as one of Barcelona's must-see landmarks. The vast white edifice with swooping ramps and glass-walled galleries almost upstages the works on display. Its location – surrounded by shabby old houses in the once rundown district of Raval – has spearheaded investment in the neighbourhood.

MACBA's extensive collection (exhibited in rotation) covers the 1940s to the 1990s, with special emphasis on Catalan and Spanish artists. It contains works by Klee, Miró and Tàpies, along with many others, including Joan Brossa, Maurizio Cattelan and Damien Hirst.

✚ 19J ✉ Plaça dels Àngels 1 ☎ 93 412 08 10 ⏰ Mon–Fri 11–7:30, Sat 10–8, Sun and public hols 10–3. Longer opening hours in summer. Guided tours in English: Mon 6pm (free) ✋ Moderate 🍴 Café (€) Ⓜ Catalunya, Universitat

MUSEU FREDERIC MARÈS

This museum was founded by local artist Frederic Marès, Spain's most prolific collector, in 1946. The entrance is via a beautiful medieval courtyard, which was once part of the Royal Palace of the Kings and Queens of Catalonia and Aragon. The museum itself is divided into three main sections: Roman artefacts in the basement, the sculpture collection on the first floor, featuring religious works from the Romanesque period to the 20th century, and the 'Sentimental Museum' on the other floors, which portrays daily life from the 15th to 20th centuries through astonishing household items. Highlights include the women's section (with collections of fans, parasols, jewellery and hat pins), the smoker's room, and the charming entertainments room, with its puppet theatres, wind-up toys and dolls.

www.museumares.bcn.es

✚ 20K or *4c* ✉ Plaça de Sant Iu 5–6 ☎ 93 310 58 00 ⏰ Tue–Sat 10–7, Sun 10–3 ✋ Moderate; free 1st Sun of month and every Wed pm 🍴 Outdoor café (€) Ⓜ Jaume I ❓ Library, shop, guided visits

MUSEU D'HISTÒRIA DE LA CIUTAT

The Museu d'Història de la Ciutat (City History Museum) is divided into several sections in various locations around the Plaça del Rei (➤ 97). To start, visitors can familiarize themselves with the earliest origins of the city by wandering around along the underground walkways beneath the square, which explore a vast area of excavations that have exposed evidence of the ancient Roman settlement of Barcino.

Casa Padellàs, a medieval mansion, was moved here stone by stone when the Via Laietana was created in 1930. Inside the mansion, carefully selected and thoroughly documented exhibits trace Barcelona's remarkable evolution through 2,000 years of history from its beginnings as a Roman trading-post to its status as a wealthy 18th-century metropolis. The highlight is the majestic barrel-vaulted banqueting hall Soló de Tinell, the seat of the first Catalan parliament, and where Ferdinand and Isabella were said to have fêted Christopher Columbus on his return from the Americas.

www.museuhistoria.bcn.es

✚ 20K or *4c* ✉ Plaça del Rei s/n ☎ 93 315 11 11 🕐 Jul–Sep Tue–Sat 10–8, Sun 10–3; Oct–Jun Tue–Sat 10–2, 4–8, Sun 10–3 ✋ Moderate; free 1st Sat afternoon of the month 🚇 Jaume I, Liceu ❓ Guided tours by appointment

PALAU GÜELL

This extraordinary building, constructed between 1886 and 1888 and declared a World Cultural Heritage site by UNESCO, was Antoni Gaudí's first major architectural project, commissioned by the Güell family.

The façade is particularly striking, with its twin arches leading into the central vestibule. Off the latter are various rooms decorated with *Modernista* fittings. A ramp leads down to the basement stables, constructed with bare-brick columns and arches. The rooftop terrace is a wonderful mixture of random spires, battlements and chimneys of differing shapes and sizes, decorated with coloured ceramic mosaics. Look closely and on one you will find a reproduction of Cobi, the 1992 Barcelona Olympics mascot. Unfortunately, the Güell family did not live here long. In 1936, the palace was confiscated by Spanish Civil War anarchists, who used it as their military headquarters and prison. It is currently closed for renovation.

✚ 19K or *1d* ✉ Carrer Nou de la Rambla 3–5 ☎ 93 317 39 74 Ⓜ Liceu

PLAÇA DE CATALUNYA

The Plaça de Catalunya is the heart of Barcelona and the hub of the city's transport system. It was first landscaped at the end of the 19th century and became of major importance as the pivotal point between the old and new city: the Barri Gòtic (▶ 86–88) to the east, the Eixample district (▶ 128–129) to the north and west, and, to the southeast, Las Ramblas (▶ 50–51) running down to the port.

Its main landmarks today are the head office of Banco Espanol de Crédito, former headquarters of the unified Socialist Party of Catalonia during the Civil War, soon to be a luxury hotel; the El Corte Inglés department store and a medley of fountains and statues, including work by important sculptors such as Gargallo, Marès and Subirachs. Today, its benches, trees and splashing fountains make it a popular place to meet and have a coffee.

✚ 20H 🍴 Several (€–€€) 🚇 Catalunya

PLAÇA DEL REI

The charming King's Square was once a bustling medieval marketplace. Today, it forms a frequent backdrop to summer open-air concerts and theatrical events, especially during the Grec festival (➤ 25), and is the location of the City History Museum (➤ 94), a huge section of which is housed in the **Palau Reial Major** (Great Royal Palace), former residence of the Counts of Barcelona.

It was on the steps leading up to the Palau Reial Major that King Ferdinand and Queen Isabella are said to have received Columbus on his return from his first voyage to America in 1493. Inside, the Spanish Inquisition once sat in the Saló del Tinell, exploiting the local myth that should any prisoner lie, the stones on the ceiling would move. Today, the hall functions as an exhibition area.

On the north side of the square is the chapel of Santa Agata (also part of the royal palace), which contains a precious 15th-century altarpiece by Jaume Huguet. On the opposite side of the square, the Palau de Lloctinent (Palace of the Deputy) was built in 1549 for the Catalan representative of the king in Madrid. A visit to the museum includes viewing an extensive swathe of the old Roman city, located underneath the palace itself.

✚ 20K or *4c* 🚇 Jaume I

Palau Reial Major

☎ 93 315 11 11 🕐 Jun–Sep Tue–Sat 10–8, Sun 10–2; Oct–May Tue–Sat 10–2, 4–8, Sun 10–3 🖐 Inexpensive ❓ Part of the Museu d'Història de la Ciutat (➤ 94)

PLAÇA REIAL

This sunny porticoed square, just off Las Ramblas, with its tall palm trees, decorative fountain and buskers was constructed in 1848. Some of the façades are decorated with terracotta reliefs of navigators and the discoverers of America, and the two tree-like central lampposts mark Gaudí's first commission in Barcelona. The pretty central fountain was inspired by the *Three Graces*.

The myriad bars that line the spacious square are popular with both locals and visitors alike, especially on summer evenings. It is advisable to keep a close watch on your belongings here – the square has a reputation for shady characters and pickpockets, hence the discreet but constant police presence. On Sunday mornings a coin and stamp market is held here.

✚ 19K or *2d* 🍴 Plenty (€–€€) 🚇 Liceu, Drassanes

PLAÇA SANT JAUME

Once the hub of Roman Barcelona, this impressive square today represents the city's political heart, and is dominated by two buildings; the neoclassical and Gothic **Casa de la Ciutat** (Town Hall) and, directly opposite, the Renaissance **Palau de la Generalitat de Catalunya** (Government of Catalonia).

The origins of Barcelona's municipal authority date back to 1249, when Jaume I granted the city the right to elect councillors, giving rise to the creation of the Consell de Cent (Council of One Hundred). The famous Saló de Cent (Chamber of One Hundred) and the black marble Saló de las Cronicas (Chamber of the Chronicles) are among the architectural highlights of the Town Hall.

➕ 20K or *3c* 🍴 Cafés (€) 🚇 Jaume I

Casa de la Ciutat/Ajuntament
☎ 010 (city hall information line) 🕒 Sun 10–1:30
✋ Free

Palau de la Generalitat de Catalunya
☎ 93 402 46 00 🕒 Guided tours every 30 mins, 10:30–1:30 every 2nd and 4th Sun of each month ✋ Free

PORT VELL

Although Barcelona was founded on sea-going tradition, for many years its seafront was in decay, until a major redevelopment prior to the 1992 Olympics reintegrated the Port Vell (Old Port) into the city by transforming it into a lively entertainment venue. The Rambla de Mar, an undulating wooden walkway and bridge, acts as an extension of Las Ramblas, connecting the city to Port Vell's many attractions.

Maremagnum, Port Vell's biggest crowd puller, is a covered shopping and entertainment centre with chic boutiques and restaurants, currently the only Sunday shopping option in Barcelona. Adjacent to the conventional cinema complex, IMAX (➤ 68) shows films in 3D, with state-of-the-art wrap-around screens and sound. Nearby is the Aquarium (➤ 68), one of the biggest and best in Europe.

Take a *golondrina* (➤ 71) for a different perspective of the harbour developments. The luxurious marina, with more than 400 berths, is one of the Mediterranean's exclusive anchorages.

✚ 20L 🖐 Free 🍴 Cafés, bars and restaurants (€–€€€) 🚇 Drassanes, Barceloneta

Golondrinas

✉ Moll de les Drassanes ☎ 93 442 31 06 🕐 Times of boat trips vary according to season 🖐 Moderate 🚇 Drassanes

LAS RAMBLAS

Best places to see, ➤ 50–51.

HOTELS

Casa Camper (€€€)

Supremely hip, urban hotel run by the famous shoe company, located in a 19th-century apartment building. All rooms comprise a sleeping and separate living area.

✉ Carrer Elisabets 11 ☎ 93 342 62 80; www.casacamper.com 🚇 Liceu

Chic&Basic (€)

White, minimalist but ultimately chic, this hotel comes with all the designer trimmings, at excellent value for money.

✉ Carrer Tallers 82 ☎ 93 302 51 83; www.chicandbasic.com 🚇 Universitat

Colón (€€–€€€)

Old-fashioned, family-friendly hotel, opposite the cathedral. It has the feel of a country home rather than that of a busy city hotel.

✉ Avenida de la Catedral 7 ☎ 93 301 14 04; www.hotelcolon.es
🚇 Jaume I, Urquinaona

Duques De Bergara (€€)

Recently renovated contemporary elegance in a turn-of-the-19th-century building with a pool.

✉ Carrer Bergara 11 ☎ 93 301 51 51; www.hotel-catalonia.com
🚇 Catalunya

Gat Raval and Gat Xino (€)

These hostels are a cut above typical backpacker accommodation, with simple, stylish rooms in bold colours, WiFi access, comfortable beds and good linen.

www.gataccommodation.com

Raval ✉ Carrer Joaquín Costa 44 ☎ 93 481 66 70 🚇 Universitat
Xino ✉ Carrer Hospital 149–155 ☎ 93 324 88 33 🚇 Liceu

Gravina (€€)

This charming 3-star hotel has a prime location near the bustling Plaça de Catalunya.

✉ Carrer Gravina 12 ☎ 93 301 68 68; www.barcelonagravinahotel.com
🚇 Universitat

Hotel 1898 (€€€)

An historic building recently made over into the only luxury hotel right on Las Ramblas, with stylish, art deco inspired rooms, spa and rooftop pool.

✉ Las Ramblas 109 ☎ 93 552 95 52; www.nnhoteles.es 🚇 Catalunya

Jardí (€)

A small, friendly hotel with clean, simple rooms. You'll pay more for a view of the Barri Gòtic's pretty squares.

✉ Plaça Sant Josep Oriol 1 ☎ 93 301 59 00; www.hoteljardi-barcelona.com
🚇 Liceu

Neri (€€€)

Tucked away in the depths of the Barri Gòtic, an 18th-century palace has been converted into one of the city's best hotels, with sumptuous Asian-inspired decorations and boasting a fashionable clientele.

✉ Carrer Sant Sever 5 ☎ 93 304 06 55; www.hotelneri.com
🚇 Jaume 1

Nouvel (€€)

This charming belle époque-style hotel is located on a pedestrianized shopping street just off Las Ramblas, and offers old-world charm and homespun comfort.

✉ Carrer Santa Anna 18–20 ☎ 93 301 82 74; www.hotelnouvel.com
🚇 Catalunya

Oriente (€€)

The Oriente was once *the* place to stay in Barcelona. Restored but still traditionally furnished, it draws those seeking a taste of history. The only downside is that it can be noisy.

✉ Las Ramblas 45 ☎ 93 302 25 58; www.husa.es 🚇 Liceu

Sant Agustí (€–€€)

Just off Las Ramblas, and near La Boqueria market, this smart, 3-star hotel offers excellent value in a quiet yet central location.

✉ Plaça Sant Agustí 3 ☎ 93 318 16 58; www.hotelsa.com 🚇 Liceu

RESTAURANTS

Agut d'Avignon (€€)

See page 62.

Bar Lobo (€€)

Large portions of *tapas*, simple Mediterranean meals and fusion food are served here to a fashionable crowd, in a trendy two-storey locale decorated with retro music posters and memorabilia.
✉ Carrer Pintor Fortuny 3 ☎ 93 481 53 46 🕐 Daily 1–5, 8–midnight
🚇 Liceu

Bar Ra (€)

Located just behind the Boqueria market, this buzzing place is best for a light Mediterranean lunch of salad, grilled fish or pasta, especially if you can secure a place on its sun-filled terrace.
✉ Plaça de la Gardunya 3 ☎ 93 423 18 78 🕐 Daily 10–4, 9:30–midnight
🚇 Liceu

La Bodega de Palma (€)

Another great local joint, this wood-lined *bodega* offers traditional *pá amb tomaquét* (rustic bread rubbed with tomato pulp) topped with all sorts of morsels such as sardines, vegetable omelette and a selection of local cheeses and cold meats.
✉ Carrer Palma de Sant Just 7 ☎ 93 315 06 56 🕐 Closed Sun 🚇 Jaume I

Café de l'Academia (€€)

One of Barcelona's best-value restaurants, with generous helpings of delicious Mediterranean cuisine in the heart of the old city.
✉ Carrer Lledó 1 ☎ 93 315 00 26 🕐 Closed weekends and 2 weeks Aug
🚇 Jaume I

Can Culleretes (€€)

One of the oldest restaurants in the city (1786), traditionally decorated with wrought-iron chandeliers. Among the highlights of the Catalan cuisine on the menu is *perdiz* (partridge) stew.
✉ Carrer Quintana 5 ☎ 93 317 30 22 🕐 Lunch: Tue–Sun 1:30–4; dinner: Tue–Sat 9–11pm; closed 3 weeks Jul 🚇 Liceu

Casa Leopoldo (€€)

Family-run seafood restaurant, in the rather run-down location of the Barri Xinés. Arrive by taxi! Its *tapas* bar is also hugely popular, with its barnacles, cuttlefish and baby eels.

✉ Carrer Sant Rafael 24 ☎ 93 441 30 14 🕐 Tue–Sat 1:30–4, 9–11, Sun 1:30–4 🚇 Liceu

L'Eucaliptus (€)

A two-storey, traditional tiled brasserie, offering a simple menu of *torradas* (toasted open sandwiches) topped with *escalivada* (traditional pepper and aubergine/eggplant dish) or salamis and Iberian ham, just off Las Ramblas.

✉ Carrer Bonsuccés 4 ☎ 93 302 18 24 🕐 Closed Sun pm and Mon 🚇 Catalunya

La Gardunya (€)

Impressive seafood platters and an excellent-value *menú del día* makes this La Boqueria market's most celebrated restaurant.

✉ Carrer Jerusalem 18 ☎ 93 302 43 23 🕐 Closed Sun 🚇 Liceu

El Gran Café (€€)

Classic restaurant, serving French and Catalan cuisine in grand turn-of-the-19th-century surroundings.

✉ Carrer d'Avinyó 9 ☎ 93 318 79 86 🕐 Closed Sun 🚇 Liceu

Juicy Jones (€)

Barcelona's vegans and vegetarians love this café for its creative, Asian-inspired dishes such as curries, dahls and other meat-free delights. It also serves fresh fruit and vegetable juices.

✉ Carrer Cardenal Casañas 7 ☎ 93 302 43 30 🕐 Daily noon–midnight 🚇 Liceu

Kynoto (€€)

This stylish sushi bar uses the best ingredients, and serves potent cocktails. Try a Tokyo Mule.

✉ Carrer Correu Vell 8 ☎ 93 268 25 40 🕐 Dinner only; closed Sun 🚇 Jaume

Mam i Teca (€€)

Cutting-edge *tapas* and regional dishes with a twist are served in this tiny white space that also boasts an excellent wine list.

✉ Carrer Luna 4 ☎ 93 441 33 35 ⏰ Closed Tue and Sun
🚇 Sant Antoni

Meson David (€€)

Traditional dishes from all over Spain are served in this riotous restaurant and local institution. Try the *lechazo*, or succulent roast pork knuckle.

✉ Carrer Carretas 63 ☎ 93 441 59 34 ⏰ Closed Mon 🚇 Drassanes

Els Quatre Gats (€–€€)

Many famous artists and intellectuals used to gather in this popular *Modernista* café in the early 1900s. Even the menu was designed by Picasso.

✉ Carrer Montsió 3 bis ☎ 93 302 41 40 ⏰ Daily 8am–2am
🚇 Catalunya

Rita Blue (€€)

Popular bar-restaurant on a pretty Barri Gòtic square that serves Tex-Mex and Asian dishes, together with oversized margaritas, before turning into a bar-club later in the evening.

✉ Plaça Sant Agusti 3 ☎ 93 342 40 86 ⏰ Daily 8pm–1am 🚇 Liceu

Tallers 76 (€)

This bright, great-value place specializes in rice dishes, from all sorts of paellas to simple *arroz a banda* (rice cooked in fish stock). The 'continuous kitchen' makes it a good option for an early lunch or dinner.

✉ Carrer Tallers 76 ☎ 93 318 89 93 ⏰ Daily 🚇 Universitat

Taxidermista (€€)

Designer restaurant in an old taxidermist's studio, offering modern dishes such as lamb couscous or duck with truffle vinaigrette.

✉ Plaça Reial 8 ☎ 93 412 45 36 ⏰ Closed Mon and 3 weeks Aug
🚇 Liceu

CAFÉS AND *TAPAS* BARS

Bar del Pi
See page 60.

Bar Pinotxo
Located to the right of the main entrance of La Boqueria, this is the best of the market's many *tapas* bars. It's not cheap, but a lunch of cava and fresh *chiperones* (baby octopus) is memorable.

✉ Stall 466, La Boqueria, Las Ramlas 89 ☎ 93 317 17 31 🕓 Mon–Sat 6–4:30 🚇 Liceu

El Bosc de les Fades
An extraordinary café-cum-magic fairy world, decorated with fountains, toadstools and fairytale princesses.

✉ Passatge de la Banca, La Rambla 4–6 ☎ 93 317 26 49 🚇 Drassanes

Buenas Migas
If it's a caffeine and carb hit you need, this indoor-outdoor café serves all sorts of croissants, pastries and tasty focaccias, plus good coffee.

✉ Plaça Bonsuccés 6 ☎ 93 318 37 08 🕓 Daily 🚇 Liceu, Catalunya

Café de l'Òpera
See page 58.

Café Zurich
See page 58.

Celta
See page 60.

Granja M Viader
See page 59.

Hard Rock Café
A prime location for this world-famous chain.

✉ Plaça de Catalunya 21 ☎ 93 270 23 05 🚇 Catalunya

Mesón del Café
See page 59.

La Plata
See page 61.

Taller de Tapas
See page 61.

Tres Tombs
Located directly opposite the Mercat de Sant Antoni, Tres Tombs is a city institution and favourite meeting point, loved by its customers for its sun-drenched terrace and no-nonsense *tapas* and light snacks.
✉ Ronda Sant Antoni 11 ☎ 93 443 41 11 🕐 Daily 🚇 Sant Antoni

SHOPPING

CLOTHES AND ACCESSORIES

Le Boudoir
Naughty but nice underwear and lingerie are displayed in this beautiful shop decorated with luxurious velvet drapery and gilt mirrors.
✉ Carrer Canuda 21 ☎ 93 302 52 81 🚇 Liceu

Calçats Solé
Hand-made leather cowboy and riding boots, leather bags and sandals from Valencia, Menorca and beyond. Larger sizes are kept in stock.
✉ Carrer Ample 7 ☎ 93 301 69 84 🚇 Drassanes

Custo Barcelona
See page 80.

Giménez y Zuazo
Women's fashions by this designer duo are fun and colourful with distinctive, unusual designs and dazzling prints.
✉ Carrer Elisabets 20 ☎ 93 412 33 81 🚇 Catalunya

Loft Avignon

The best of international and Spain's own designer labels for men and women. If you have seen it in the fashion magazines, it's probably here.

✉ Carrer Avinyó ☎ 93 301 24 20 🚇 Jaume I

Mango

This branch of the international chain brims with inexpensive, trendy designs for the truly fashion conscious. There are several branches around Barcelona, include a particularly large one at Passeig de Gràcia 65 and another inside the Maremagnum shopping mall.

✉ Avinguda Portal de l'Àngel 7 ☎ 93 317 69 85 🚇 Catalunya

Maremagnum

At the port end of Las Ramblas across the wooden swing bridge, Maremagnum is a mall with a location. Fashion dominates, from Spanish staples such as Mango to more eclectic shoe and accessory shops. Afterwards, take in the sea views at one of the many outdoor cafés.

✉ Port Vell s/n ⏰ Daily 10–10 🚇 Drassanes

Vialis

In a city full of great shoe stores, this one stands out for its unusual styling and interesting textures and colours. They are comfortable too.

✉ Carrer Elisabets 20 ☎ 93 342 60 71 🚇 Liceu

Zara

See page 81.

CRAFTS, ART AND DESIGN
Alamacenes de Pilar

This rambling old warehouse outlet sells beautiful fans, combs, shawls and other Spanish accessories for that authentic *señorita* look.

✉ Carrer Boqueria 43 ☎ 93 317 79 84 🚇 Liceu

Art Escudellers

Huge emporium selling Spanish pottery and ceramics, from factory pieces to arty individual designs. In the basement are a wine cellar, delicatessen and wine bar where you can sample the local products.

✉ Carrer Escudellers 23 ☎ 93 412 68 01 🚇 Liceu, Drassanes

Cereria Subirà

The oldest shop in the city of Barcelona, founded in 1761, selling candles of all sorts, ancient and modern, for both religious and purely practical purposes.

✉ Baixada Llibreteria 7 ☎ 93 315 26 06 🚇 Jaume I

Cosas de Casa

Hand-made patchwork quilts and fabrics, including the distinctive Mallorcan *roba de llengües* (literally 'cloth of tongues'), striking for its red, blue or green zigzag patterns.

✉ Plaça Sant Josep Oriol 5 ☎ 93 302 73 28 🚇 Jaume I, Liceu

Germanes Garcia

Wickerwork of all shapes and sizes tumbles out of this village-style shop into the streets of the Old City.

✉ Carrer Banys Nous 15 ☎ 93 318 66 46 🚇 Liceu

El Ingenio

Children adore this old-fashioned magic shop, where party tricks are sold, and carnival masks and costumes are created in a workshop at the back. Come here for free magic shows on Thursday afternoons. A real Aladdin's cave and child's (or inner child's) delight.

✉ Carrer Rauric 6 ☎ 93 317 71 38 🚇 Liceu, Jaume I

La Manual Alpargatera

All kinds of hand-made, straw-woven items are on sale here, including hats, bags and their speciality, espadrilles. They are a great souvenir.

✉ Carrer Avinyó 7 ☎ 93 301 01 72 🚇 Liceu, Jaume I

Sala Parés
Barcelona's finest gallery specializes in 19th- and 20th-century paintings, drawings and sculptures.
✉ Carrer Pextritxol 5 ☎ 93 318 70 08 Ⓜ Liceu

FOOD AND DRINK
Casa Colomina
Turron, which is like nougat, from Valencia is the speciality here, sold by the slice or bar. It can made with a number of flavours. Delicious!
✉ Carrer Cucurulla 2 ☎ 93 317 46 81 Ⓜ Liceu

Formatgeria La Seu
This old dairy now specializes in rare Spanish cheeses and olive oils, with small tables at the back so you can taste before you buy.
✉ Carrer Dagueria 16 ☎ 93 412 65 48 Ⓜ Jaume I

Papabubble
This old-fashioned sweet shop makes lollypops, candy canes and other sticky snacks right in front of your eyes.
✉ Carrer Ample 28 ☎ 93 268 86 25 Ⓜ Jaume I

Vins i Caves La Catedral
You will be able to choose from wines stocked from all over Spain, with a particularly strong selection from Catalonia. They make a good gift.
✉ Plaça de Ramon Berenguer el Gran 1 ☎ 93 319 07 27 Ⓜ Jaume I

MUSIC, BOOKS AND ANTIQUES
L'Arca de l'Avìa
A treasure trove of antique cottons, linens, silks. Beautiful, albeit pricey, patchwork eiderdowns and beaded bags.
✉ Carrer Banys Nous 20 ☎ 93 302 15 98 Ⓜ Liceu

Artur Ramon Anticuario
A wide array of antique paintings, sculpture and decorative arts.
✉ Carrer de la Palla 25 ☎ 93 302 59 70 Ⓜ Jaume I

Casa Beethoven
Founded in 1915, this shop has scores and sheet music, specializing in pieces by Spanish and Catalan composers.
✉ La Rambla 97 ☎ 93 301 48 26 Ⓜ Liceu

Castelló
A chain of record shops. Carrer Tallers 3 has a huge selection of pop, rock, jazz, blues and soul. The shop at No 7 is devoted to classical music.
✉ Carrer Tallers 3 & 7 ☎ 93 302 59 46 Ⓜ Catalunya

La Central
Enormous, two-storey bookshop with a large section of English-language literature and a lovely café.
✉ Carrer Elisabets 6 ☎ 93 317 02 93 Ⓜ Catalunya

FNAC
See page 80.

Jordi Capell – Cooperative d'Arquitectes
Specialist bookshop for architecture and design, in the basement of the College of Architects.
✉ Plaça Nova 5 ☎ 93 481 35 60 Ⓜ Jaume I, Liceu

ENTERTAINMENT

City Hall
Just near the Plaça Catalunya, this established dance club is guaranteed to be full any night of the week. Music changes from funk on weeknights to heavy-duty techno at weekends.
✉ Rambla Catalunya 2–4 ☎ 93 317 21 77 ⏰ Daily midnight–5am Ⓜ Catalunya

Club Fellini
A hugely popular dance club right on Las Ramblas, pulling in a mixed crowd of locals, students and tourists all ready to get down to the ear-splitting funk and techno.
✉ Las Ramblas 27 ☎ 93 272 49 80 ⏰ Daily midnight–5am Ⓜ Drassanes

Harlem Jazz Club

Small, but very atmospheric jazz club – a favourite of jazz aficionados.

✉ Carrer Comtessa de Sobradiel 8 ☎ 93 310 07 55 🕐 Tue–Sun 8pm–4am
Ⓜ Jaume I

Jamboree

A choice nightspot for blues, soul, jazz, funk and occasional hip-hop live bands. Later on, upstairs is a laid-back bar with Spanish music.

✉ Plaça Reial ☎ 93 301 75 64 🕐 Daily 9pm–5am; live gigs start at 11pm
Ⓜ Liceu

La Macarena

Dark and steamy disco club that pulls in an energetic crowd.

✉ Carrer Nou de Sant Francesc 5 ☎ 93 302 45 93 🕐 Mon–Sat midnight–5am Ⓜ Drassanes

Marsella

A traditional bar in the Barri Xines, run by the same family for five generations, serving locally made *absenta* (absinthe).

✉ Carrer Sant Pau 65 ☎ 93 442 72 63 🕐 Mon–Thu 10pm–2:30am, Fri–Sun 10pm–3:30am Ⓜ Liceu

THEATRE AND CINEMA

Gran Teatre del Liceu

World-famous singers, including the Catalan diva Montserrat Caballé, have performed here.

✉ Las Ramblas 51–59 ☎ 93 485 99 13; www.liceubarcelona.com
Ⓜ Liceu

IMAX Cinema

See page 68.

SPORT

Fat Tire Bike Tours

See page 71.

La Ribera to Port Olímpic

La Ribera, one of the oldest districts of Barcelona, has become home to buzzing *tapas* bars, wine bars and stylish restaurants situated in Gothic palaces, and also has the city's most eclectic shopping opportunities.

The northern half of the district, Sant Pere, contains the Modernist masterpiece Palau de la Música Catalana. Carrer de Montcada, in the Born, is now a showcase of art galleries and museums, including the Museu Picasso, one of the city's biggest attractions. The lanes around Carrer de Montcada are full of

workshops where jewellers and potters carry on their trade much as they did in medieval times.

Passeig del Born, the main thoroughfare through the Born district, is a lively promenade lined with restaurants and cocktail bars. Here you'll find the Basílica de Santa Maria del Mar, known as the merchant's cathedral. A pleasant waterfront walk leads from La Ribera around the fishing village of Barceloneta to the popular beaches on either side of Port Olímpic.

LA BARCELONETA AND PORT OLÍMPIC

Following the siege and conquest of Barcelona by Felipe V in 1714, a large area of the Ribera district was destroyed to make way for a new citadel. The displaced residents lived for years in makeshift shelters on the beach, until in 1755 a new district was developed on a triangular wedge of reclaimed land between the harbour and the sea, named La Barceloneta (Little Barcelona).

In the 19th century, La Barceloneta became home to seamen and dockers and it is still a working district, retaining its shanty-town atmosphere, fishy smells and a quayside lined with the boats. Today visitors come here to eat in the fine seafood eateries, in particular those along the main thoroughfare, Passeig Joan de Borbó, and the restaurants of the converted Palau de Mar warehouse (➤ 116–117).

By contrast, Port Olímpic, with its stylish promenades and glittering marina, has given new impetus to Barcelona's nautical activities. Its chic restaurants, cafés and bars have become a lively nightspot popular with both locals and tourists alike. Spain's two tallest buildings preside over the port – the office-filled Torre Mapfre and the five-star hotel Arts Barcelona, Barcelona's top hotel (➤ 121). Nearby, a striking bronze fish sculpture by Frank Gehry (architect of the Guggenheim Museum in Bilbao) heralds the start of the Passeig Marítim, which links the port with La Barceloneta and then extends 8km (5 miles) to Sant Adrià del Besòs.

✚ 21L (Barceloneta), 23M (Port Olímpic) 🍴 Plenty (€–€€€) 🚇 Barceloneta, Ciutadella/Vila Olímpica, Poble Nou 🚌 Barceloneta: 17, 36, 39, 40, 45, 57, 59, 64, 157. Port Olímpic: 10, 45, 57, 59, 71, 92, 157

MUSEU D'HISTÒRIA DE CATALUNYA

Thanks to the influence of the Olympic Games, and the opening up of the old port as a leisure area, the Palau de Mar (Palace of the Sea) – an impressive late 19th-century warehouse – became the centrepiece of a harbourside development that includes a promenade, restaurants and marina. It houses the Museu d'Història de Catalunya (Museum of Catalan History).

This is one of Barcelona's most interactive museums, opened in 1996. Some critics have dubbed it a 'theme park', because of its lack of original exhibits, but it is nevertheless a dynamic and stimulating museum, covering the history of Catalonia in an entertaining fashion, through state-of-the-art displays, films, special effects and audiovisual technology – tread an Arab waterwheel, mount a cavalier's charger, drive an early tram, take cover in a Civil War air-raid shelter…

The museum is divided into seven sections, each presenting an in-depth picture of the economy, politics, technology, culture and everyday life of Catalonia over the centuries: the region's prehistory, the consolidation of Catalonia in the Middle Ages, its maritime role, links with the Austrian Empire in the 16th and 17th centuries, economic growth and industrialization, the 1936 Civil War and the repression of Catalonia under Franco, through to the restoration of democracy in 1979. The museum gives an insight into the complexities of this 'nation within a nation'.

www.mhcat.net

✚ 21L   ✉ Plaça Pau Vila 3, Port Vell   ☎ 93 225 47 00   🕐 Tue–Sat 10–7,

Wed 10–8, Sun and public hols 10–2:30 🖐 Moderate; free 1st Sun of month
🍴 Rooftop café (€) 🚇 Barceloneta ❓ Gift shop, temporary exhibitions

MUSEU PICASSO
Best places to see, ➤ 46–47.

MUSEU TÈXTIL I D'INDUMENTÀRIA
The Museu Tèxtil i d'Indumentària (Textile and Clothing Museum)
acts as a reminder of how, thanks to its thriving textile industry,
Barcelona rose to prosperity in the 1800s. It occupies a beautiful
14th-century palace, in what would then have been the
aristocratic heart of Barcelona.

The museum collections include textiles, tapestries, lace and
clothes from medieval to modern times, with displays of textile
machinery, dolls, shoes and other fashion accessories.
www.museutextil.bcn.es

➕ 21K ✉ Carrer Montcada 12–14 ☎ 93 319 76 03 🕐 Tue–Sat 10–6,
Sun and public hols 10–3 🖐 Moderate 🍴 Café-restaurant (€) 🚇 Jaume I

PALAU DE LA MÚSICA CATALANA

In a city bursting with architectural wonders, the Palau de la Música Catalana (Palace of Catalan Music) – commissioned by the Orfeó Català (Catalan Musical Society) in 1904 and created by local architect Lluís Domènech i Montaner between 1905 and 1908 – stands out as one of Barcelona's greatest masterpieces and a symbol of the renaissance of Catalan culture. In 1997 it was declared a World Heritage Site by UNESCO.

The bare brick façade is highlighted with colourful ceramic pillars, fancy windows and busts of Palestrina, Bach, Beethoven and Wagner. The sculptural group projecting from the corner of the building represents popular song. A balcony runs around the building and the main structure is supported by ornate columns that form huge dramatic archways over the entrance.

The interior continues the ornamental theme with a profusion of decoration in the entrance hall, foyer and staircase – almost overpowering in its attention to detail. The *pièce de résistance*, however, must be the concert hall, with its exquisite roof (an inverted cupola made of stained glass), its sculptures, ceramics and paintings dedicated to musical muses (including Josep Anselm Clavé, the great 19th-century reviver of Catalan music), and its beautiful balconies and columns, designed to enhance the perspective of the auditorium.

It's no surprise that this is one of the city's main venues for classical music, and, until the restoration of the Liceu Opera House and the opening of the Auditorium, was home to two orchestras, the Liceu and the Orquestra Simfònica de Barcelona i Nacional de Catalunya. It's a memorable experience to attend one of the nightly concerts; the acoustics are excellent.

www.palaumusica.org

➕ 21J ✉ Carrer Sant Francesc de Paula 2 ☎ 90 244 28 82 🕐 Daily 10–3:30 💵 Expensive 🚇 Urquinaona ❓ Entrance (except for performances) by guided tour only; purchase tickets for tours (in advance) from La Muses del Palau gift shop (adjacent) or the ticket office if open

PARC DE LA CIUTADELLA

This delightful walled park is a haven of shade and tranquillity just a stone's throw from the old city and waterfront. What's more, hidden among the trees, lawns, promenades and a boating lake, you'll find the Parc Zoològic (➤ 69) and a host of other attractions.

In 1888 the park was the site of the Universal Exposition and still contains some impressive relics of that great fair, including a striking *Modernista* café which now houses the **Museu de Zoologia,** with highlights that include a fascinating Whale Room and a Sound Library of recordings of animal sounds. Nearby, the neoclassical **Museu de Geologia,** with its rare and valuable minerals, fossils and rocks, opened in 1878 as Barcelona's first public museum. The main showpiece of the park is the Font Monumental – a huge, neoclassical-style fountain, smothered in allegorical sculptures.

✚ 22K ✉ Main entrance: Passeig Lluís Companys 🖐 Free 🚇 Ciutadella, Arc de Triomf, Barceloneta, Jaume I

Museu de Ciencias Naturales

✉ Passeig de Picasso ☎ 93 319 69 12 🕐 Thu, Sat 10–6:30, Tue, Wed, Fri, Sun 10–2:30 🖐 Moderate (joint ticket)

SANTA MARIA DEL MAR

Best places to see, ➤ 54–55.

VILA OLÍMPICA

Just behind Port Olímpic, part of the rundown district of Poble Nou was developed into the Vila Olímpica – home to 15,000 competitors during the 1992 Olympic Games. It is now a high-tech corridor of apartment blocks, shops and offices.

✚ 23M ✉ Vila Olímpica 🚇 Ciutadella 🚌 36, 45, 59

HOTEL

Arts Barcelona (€€€)

Hotel Arts Barcelona, a 44-storey hotel, towers above the entrance to the Port Olímpic. Its post-Modern interior is filled with modern Catalan art and on its waterfront terraces a vast copper fish designed by Frank Gehry (➤ 78, 115) is a symbol of the city. This fashionable hotel provides state-of-the-art, unabashed luxury beside the sea, and has a spa on the 42nd floor, which was opened to celebrate the hotel's tenth anniversary.

✉ Carrer de la Marina 19–21 ☎ 93 221 10 00; www.ritzcarlton.com
Ⓜ Ciutadella/Vila Olímpica

RESTAURANTS

Abac (€€€)

The elegance, spaciousness and minimalism of Abac's stylish cream-and-orange dining room provides a perfect backdrop for the fine Spanish haute cuisine of local chef Xavier Pellicier.

✉ Carrer Rec 79–89 ☎ 93 319 66 00 🕐 Closed Sun Ⓜ Barceloneta

Agua (€€)

Located right on Barceloneta beach, near Port Olímpic. The menu is creative, yet offers excellent traditional Barceloneta fare, with the emphasis on rice-based dishes. Sunday lunchtime is popular.

✉ Passeig Marítim de la Barceloneta 30 ☎ 93 225 12 72 Ⓜ Ciutadella-Vila Olímpica

Bestial (€€)

This fabulous Italian bistro is right by the Hotel Arts Barcelona, with extensive wood decking, palm trees and parasol topped tables. There are impressive views from the huge glass façade and terrace of Frank Gehry's golden fish.

✉ Passeig Marítim 32 ☎ 93 224 04 07 🕐 Daily Ⓜ Ciutadella-Vila Olímpica

La Bombeta (€)

A genuine, old-school *tapas* bar worth seeking out. The speciality is *bombas*, huge fluffy potato balls smothered in spicy *brava* sauce.

✉ Carrer Maquinista 3 ☎ 93 319 94 45 🕐 Closed Wed Ⓜ Barceloneta

Can Majó (€€€)
See page 62.

Comerç 24 (€€€)
One of the leading names in 'New Catalan Cuisine', Carles Abellan redefines classic Spanish dishes, with combinations, textures and flavours that delight and often confound. Try the *festa de tapas* (tasting menu) for the full experience.

✉ Carrer Comerç 24 ☎ 93 319 21 02 🕐 Closed Sun, Mon 🚇 Jaume I

La Gavina (€€€)
One of the best of a stylish strip of seafood restaurants overlooking the water. There are plenty of fish dishes to choose from, including fresh mussels and an excellent seafood based paella (for two).

✉ Palau de Mar, Plaça Pau Vila 1 ☎ 93 221 20 41 🕐 Daily 🚇 Barceloneta

Hofmann (€€€)
Interpretations of regional dishes by Mey Hofmann, one of Spain's most talented chefs, who also runs a world-renowned cookery school on the premises.

✉ Carrer Argenteria 74–78 ☎ 93 218 71 65 🕐 Mon–Sat 1:30–3:15, 9–11; closed Sun, Aug 🚇 Jaume I ❓ Phone ahead for details of special two-day cookery courses

Mosquito (€)
For something a little different, this simple, friendly place offers Asian-inspired *platillos* (small plates) which are best shared in a large group. The dahl salad and Thai-style spring rolls are excellent.

✉ Carrer Carders 46 ☎ 93 268 75 69 🕐 Closed Sun, Mon 🚇 Arc de Triomf

El Passadís d'en Pep (€€€)
There's no menu as such here, just some of the best fish in town. Choose from bream, bass, oysters, shellfish or the catch of the day.

✉ Pla del Palau 2 ☎ 93 310 10 21 🕐 Closed Sun, Mon lunch, Aug 🚇 Barceloneta

El Rey de la Gamba (€€)

The 'King of Prawns' serves seafood and cured hams and comprises two adjacent restaurants. It can be very busy at weekends.

✉ Passeig Joan de Borbó 53 ☎ 93 225 64 00 🕐 Tue–Sun 1pm–midnight 🚇 Barceloneta

Sal Cafè (€€)

Located right on the waterfront promenade, Sal Cafè offers Mediterranean cuisine as bright as its surroundings. Reserve ahead for an outdoor table, where you can take in the sea view under the shade of an enormous orange umbrella, the restaurant's trademark.

✉ Passeig Marítimo de la Barceloneta s/n ☎ 93 224 07 07 🕐 Sun–Wed 1:30–4, Thu–Sat 1:30–4, 8:30–midnight 🚇 Barceloneta

Senyor Parellada (€€)

This long-standing restaurant is a neighbourhood favourite serving excellent Mediterranean cuisine and Catalan fare in classically stylish surroundings. Try the *botifarra* (Catalan sausage) with *mongetes* (white beans) followed by *crema catalana* (crème brûlée).

✉ Carrer Argenteria 37 ☎ 93 310 50 94 🕐 Daily 🚇 Jaume I

Set Portes (€€€)

See page 63.

CAFÉS AND *TAPAS* BARS

Cafè Hotel Arts

Located inside the Picasso Museum (➤ 46), though with a separate entrance, this charming café serves light food and refreshments either inside in a pretty dining room of wrought-iron furniture or on an outdoor, inner-courtyard patio.

✉ Carrer Montcada 15–23 ☎ 93 310 31 38 🕐 Closed Mon 🚇 Jaume I

Cal Pep

See page 60.

Origins 99.9%
This is the original and prettiest of a chain of cafés using Catalan-only ingredients. Cakes, sandwiches and salads are all top quality and there is a shop selling cheeses and other local specialities.
✉ Carrer Vidrería 6–8 ☎ 93 310 75 31 🕐 Daily 🚇 Jaume I

Sagardi
See page 61.

Santa Marta
On the beachfront, this bohemian café is great for lazing on the terrace, enjoying a coffee or a drink later in the evening. On Sunday evenings there is live acoustic music and during the day free WiFi.
✉ Grau i Torres 59 ☎ 69 223 68 01 🕐 Daily 🚇 Barceloneta

Taller de Tapas
See page 61.

Tèxtil Cafè
See page 59.

La Vinya del Senyor
Tiny, stand-up wine bar, with terrace, beside Santa Maria del Mar.
✉ Plaça Santa Maria 5 ☎ 93 310 33 79 🕐 Closed Mon 🚇 Jaume I

SHOPPING

ARTS, CRAFTS AND DESIGN

Alamacen Marabi
Beautiful handmade felt toys and other items from small finger-puppets to giant teddy bears.
✉ Carrer Flassaders 30 bis ☎ No phone 🚇 Jaume I

Galeria Maeght
Come to these specialists in 20th-century art, design and photography for posters, prints and other graphic works. Upstairs is a prestigious art gallery.
✉ Carrer Montcada 25 ☎ 93 301 42 54 🚇 Jaume I

El Rey de la Màgica

Stepping inside this extraordinary magic shop, founded in 1881 is like entering another world.

✉ Carrer la Princessa 11 ☎ 93 319 73 93 🚇 Jaume I

BOOKS, MUSIC AND ANTIQUES

Norma Comics

Barcelona's largest comic shop sells a huge variety of comics from many different genres.

✉ Passeig de Sant Joan 9 ☎ 93 244 84 23 🚇 Arc de Triomf

CLOTHES AND ACCESSORIES

Alea

Splendid showcase for up-and-coming Catalan jewellers in the trendy district of La Ribera.

✉ Carrer Argenteria 66 ☎ 93 310 13 73 🚇 Jaume I, Barceloneta

Custo Barcelona

See page 80.

On-Land

Highly fashionable yet ultimately wearable clothing for men and women from Spanish designers.

✉ Carrer Princesa 25 ☎ 93 310 02 11 🚇 Jaume I

FOOD AND DRINK

Brunells Pastisseria

Appears in the *Guinness Book of Records* for making Spain's biggest Easter egg. Try the *torró* (traditional almond fudge), *roques de Montserrat* (meringues) and *carquinyolis* (soft almond biscuits). There is also a café on site.

✉ Carrer Montcada 7 ☎ 93 319 68 25 🚇 Jaume I

Casa Gispert

Dried fruits, spices, cocoa, coffee and nuts which are toasted daily in a traditional oak-fired oven.

✉ Carrer Sombrerers 23 ☎ 93 319 75 35 🚇 Jaume I

ENTERTAINMENT

CDLC
Owned by the Barça football team, one of the most exclusive (and expensive) clubs in the city. There's a dance floor, beachfront terrace and a restaurant serving light Mediterranean cuisine.
✉ Passeig Maritim 32 ☎ 93 224 04 70 🕔 Daily until 3am 🚇 Ciutadella-Vila Olímpica

Club Catwalk
Two separate dance floors, one playing house and the other R&B and hip hop. Expect celebrity DJs and a hefty admission.
✉ Carrer Ramon Trias Fargas s/n ☎ 93 221 61 61 🕔 Thu–Sat until 5am
🚇 Ciutadella-Vila Olímpica

Gimlet
An established cocktail bar popular for its New York vibe, jazz soundtrack and excellently mixed drinks.
✉ Carrer Rec 24 ☎ 93 310 10 27 🕔 Closed Sun 🚇 Jaume I

Mix
Fashionable bar-club with stylish decor and clientele to match. There is live jazz on Wednesday and DJs spinning smooth background music other nights of the week.
✉ Carrer Comerç 21 ☎ 93 319 46 96 🕔 Daily until 3am 🚇 Jaume I

Palau de la Música Catalana
Barcelona's main venue for classical music (➤ 118–119).
✉ Carrer Sant Francesc de Paula 2 ☎ 93 295 72 00; www.palaumusica.org
🕔 Box office: Mon–Fri 10–9, Sat 3–9

SPORT

SAILING
Base Nàutica de la Mar Bella
Friendly sailing school that also rents catamarans and windsurfers by the hour.
✉ Avinguda Litoral in the port Mar Bella ☎ 93 221 04 32; wwwbasenautica.org 🚇 Ciutadella-Villa Olímpica

The Eixample and Gràcia

At the heart of the Eixample is the famed 'Golden Square', an area of elegant streets lined with *Modernista* architecture ranging from private homes to public buildings, two of them by Gaudí: Casa Milà and Casa Batlló. The Eixample is also where you will find Gaudí's amazing unfinished La Sagrada Família, one of the city's most celebrated sights.

Park Güell

GRÀCIA

L'EIXAMPLE

Gràcia, once an outlying village, is now a picturesque suburb. It is home to students, artists and writers and its atmosphere, narrow streets and shady squares contrast sharply with the orderly grid plan of fashionable Eixample. Gràcia also has a building by Gaudí – Casa Vicens.

CASA ASIA

This sumptuous *Modernista* mansion by Doménech i Montaner
houses Barcelona's Asian cultural centre, regularly hosting
exhibitions which make it well worth visiting. These can range from
ancient Tibetan art and craft to Vietnamese propaganda posters
and the work of Asian photographers, and are heightened by their
magnificent setting. Every September Casa Asia organizes the
Festival Asia, which invites Asian artists and performers to the city.
www.casaasia.es

🚹 8F ✉ Avinguda Diagonal 373 ☎ 93 238 73 37 🕐 Tue–Sat 10–8, Sun
10–2 🖐 Free 🍴 Snack bar Ⓜ Diagonal

CASA MILÀ (LA PEDRERA)

Best places to see, ➤ 36–37.

L'EIXAMPLE

L'Eixample means 'The Extension' in Catalan, and this district was laid out between 1860 and 1920 to expand the city beyond its medieval walls and link it with outlying municipalities.

The innovative plan, drawn up by civil engineer Ildefons Cerdà, broke with the tradition of Spanish urban planning, with its geometric grid of streets running parallel to the seafront. The aptly named Avinguda Diagonal cuts through at 45 degrees to add a touch of originality. The utopian features of Cerdà's plan have been largely forgotten, and today many people dislike its monotony while others praise its visionary urban planning.

The Eixample consists of two *barris*: *L'Esquerra* (The Left) is more residential, whereas *La Dreta* (The Right) contains the *Modernista* landmarks Casa Milà, the three properties of La Manzana de la Discòrdia, the Fundació Antoni Tàpies, the Hospital de la Santa Creu i Sant Pau and La Sagrada Família. Chic boutiques line its streets and, at night, its stylish bars and nightclubs come alive.

✚ 19G ⑪ Plenty (€–€€€) ⑧ Catalunya, Diagonal, Entença, Girona, Hospital Clínic, Passeig de Gràcia, Provença, Tetuan, Vergaguer, Universitat

FUNDACIÓ ANTONI TÀPIES

The Tàpies Foundation was established by Catalan artist Antoni Tàpies in 1984 to promote the study and understanding of modern art. It is housed in the former Montaner i Simon publishing house, built by Lluís Domènech i Montaner between 1880 and 1889. The striking *Mudejar*-style façade is crowned by an eye-catching piece of art made of wire and tubing by Tàpies, titled *Cloud and Chair* (1990). Inside, there is an exhaustive library documenting art and artists of the 20th century, and one of the most complete collections of Tàpies' own works.

www.fundaciotapies.org

✚ 20G ✉ Carrer d'Aragó 255 ☎ 93 487 03 15 🕓 Tue–Sun 10–8
✋ Moderate, children under 16 free 🚌 7, 16, 17, 20, 22, 24, 28, 39, 43, 44
🚇 Passeig de Gràcia ❓ Library and small bookshop

GRÀCIA

In 1820, Gràcia was a mere village of about 2,500 inhabitants. By 1897, the population had swollen to 61,000, making it the ninth-largest city in Spain, known as a radical centre of Catalanism and anarchism. This is reflected in some street names – Mercat de la Llibertat and Plaça de la

Revolució. Since then, Gràcia has been engulfed by the expanding city, yet even now it maintains a village-like, no-frills, bohemian atmosphere and the *Graciencs* still call the cityfolk *Barcelonins*.

There are no real 'tourist' attractions here, except Gaudí's first major commission, Casa Vicens

(Carrer de les Carolines 24), still a private home. Gràcia's real appeal is its muddle of narrow atmospheric streets and squares, including the Plaça del Sol, an ideal place to stop for a coffee and watch the world go by. The Plaça de la Virreina and the Plaça de Rius i Taulet are two of the oldest squares. You'll also find great shopping along the Carrer Verdi and a concentration of reasonably priced bars and restaurants in Gràcia.

➕ 9E 🍴 Plenty (€–€€€) Ⓜ Fontana, Gràcia, Joanic ❓ *Festa Major* every August (► 25)

HOSPITAL DE LA SANTA CREU I SANT PAU

This remarkable hospital complex is a masterpiece of *Modernisme* by innovative architect Lluís Domènech i Montaner. Not only did he deliberately defy the orderliness of the Eixample by aligning the buildings at 45 degrees to the street grid, but he also built the complex in contravention of established hospital concepts by creating a 'hospital-village' of 48 small pavilions connected by underground passages and surrounded by gardens, rather than one single massive building.

Construction began in 1902, as a long-overdue replacement for the old hospital in the Raval, following a bequest from a Catalan banker called Pau Gil. The new hospital was inaugurated in 1930. The main pavilion, with its graceful tower and ornate mosaic façade, serves as a majestic entrance to the whole ensemble. Inside, the various pavilions are grouped around gardens that occupy an area equivalent to nine blocks of the Eixample, where both doctors and patients alike can enjoy a peaceful natural environment. The pavilions are decorated in ornate *Modernista* style using brick, colourful ceramics and natural stone.

Over the years, the hospital complex has been restored several times and in 1984 it was declared a World Cultural Heritage site by UNESCO.

www.rutadelmodernisme.com

✚ 12E ✉ Carrer de Sant Antoni Maria Claret 167–171 ☎ 90 207 66 21 🕐 Guided tours in English Mon–Thu 10:15 and 12:15 ✋ Moderate; grounds free 🍴 Small coffee shop in one of the pavilions (€) 🚇 Hospital de Sant Pau ❓ Please remember that this is a hospital and not just a tourist attraction

MANZANA DE LA DISCORDIA

Casa Amatller

This is the first of three houses that have striking *Modernista* façades and are collectively known as the Manzana de la Discordia. Chocolate manufacturer Antonio Amatller i Costa commissioned Josep Puig i Cadafalch to remodel Casa Amatller into an extravagant home with a neo-Gothic façade decorated with sculptures, coats of arms and floral reliefs, and crowned by a stepped gable. Inside the broad entranceway, the beautiful wooden elevator was one of the earliest to be installed in Barcelona. Note also the amazing carvings on one interior doorway depicting animals making chocolate. To see inside the building you will need to take a guided tour, which includes an opportunity to taste Amatller chocolate.

www.amatller.org

🚇 20G ✉ Passeig de Gràcia 41 ☎ 93 487 72 17 🕐 Guided tours Mon–Fri at 11, 12 and 1. Advance reservations advised ✋ Moderate 🚇 Passeig de Gràcia ❓ The entrance hall, open to the public, contains information on the city's *Modernista* attractions (free)

Casa Batlló

Casa Batlló is one of the most famous buildings of the *Modernista* school, designed by Gaudí for Josep Batlló i Casanovas and completed in 1907. It is said to illustrate the triumph of Sant Jordi (St George) over the dragon, with its mosaic façade,

covered in glazed blue, green and ochre ceramics, representing the scaly skin of the dragon, its knobbly roof the dragon's back, the tower the saint's cross and the wave-like balconies the skulls and bones of victims. A visit of the interior gives an insight into Gaudí's designs, and takes in an apartment, the attic and roof terrace.
www.casabatllo.es

🚇 20G ✉ Passeig de Gràcia 43 ☎ 93 216 03 06 🕐 Daily 9–8 ✋ Expensive
Ⓜ Passeig de Gràcia

Casa Lleó-Morera

This striking building is considered Lluís Domènech i Montaner's most exuberant decorative work. Its flamboyant façade cleverly minimizes its corner plot by placing visual emphasis on the distinctive ornate circular balconies, columned galleries and oriel windows. Inside, a florid pink mosaic vestibule and open staircase lead to first-floor living quarters, which are lavishly decorated with stencilled stuccowork, stained glass, marquetry and mosaics, portraying roses (the nationalist symbol of Catalonia), lions *(lleó)* and mulberry bushes *(morera)* which give this house its name. The interior is closed to the public, but the exterior is well worth a visit.

🚇 20G ✉ Passeig de Gràcia 35 ☎ No phone 🕐 Interior not open to the public Ⓜ Passeig de Gràcia

MUSEU EGIPCI DE BARCELONA

Although some of the pieces in the expansive Egyptian collection belonging to the owner of the Derby Hotels can be seen in the Claris and Hotel Balmes (➤ 139), the bulk of them are here at this impressive museum. From beautifully carved

sarcophagi to everyday utensils, sculpture, jewellery and mummified animals, the well-ordered exhibits are spread out over two floors of this pretty Eixample mansion and span more than 3,000 years of fascinating Egyptian culture.

There are special night visits during summer during in which actors dressed in full Egyptian regalia perform scenes from Cleopatra's life, ending in a banquet held on the rear terrace.

www.fundclos.com

➕ 20G ✉ Carrer Valencia 284 ☎ 93 488 01 88 ⏰ Closed Sun afternoon ✋ Moderate 🚇 Passeig de Gràcia ❓ Book and gift shop

PARC DE LA CREUETA DEL COLL

This park was built in a former quarry by Olympic architects Martorell and Mackay in 1987. Surrounded by dramatic cliff-faces, it is scattered with modern sculptures and wooded pathways. A sand-fringed swimming pool is popular with children in summer.

✚ 10B ✉ Passeig Mare de Déu del Coll 🕓 Daily 10–dusk ✋ Free
🚌 25, 28, 87

PARK GÜELL

Best places to see, ➤ 48–49.

LA SAGRADA FAMÍLIA

Best places to see, ➤ 52–53.

TORRE AGBAR

Barcelona's brazen new structure is a colourful landmark on the skyline. Built for the local water company by French architect Jean Nouvel, the Torre Agbar features an ingenious aluminium 'skin' that ripples with light at night in hues of green, blue and red.

www.torreagbar.com

✚ 24H (off map) ✉ Plaça de les Glories s/n 🚇 Glories

HOTELS

Hotel Balmes (€€)

It's not all five-star prices in the Eixample. This great little hotel offers comfort and a rear garden with a pool, a real rarity for a three-star hotel. It's located within walking distance of the Passeig de Gràcia shopping strip and all the major sites.

✉ Carrer Mallorca 216 ☎ 93 451 19 14; www.derbyhotels.com 🚇 Diagonal

Claris (€€€)

Just off the exclusive Passeig de Gràcia, this impressive hotel features modern accommodation furnished in marble, glass and works of art. There are several restaurants, a roof terrace with pool, a fitness centre, a Japanese garden and even a museum of priceless Egyptian antiques.

✉ Carrer Pau Clarís 150 ☎ 93 487 62 62; www.derbyhotels.com 🚇 Passeig de Gràcia

Condes De Barcelona (€€€)

Stylish hotel that puts you right at the heart of Barcelona's main shopping district. Elegant public rooms, and bedrooms furnished in *Modernista* style.

✉ Passeig de Gràcia 73–75 ☎ 93 445 00 00 🚇 Diagonal

Hotel Palace (€€€)

Another member of the 'Leading Hotels of the World' group, this hotel has gracious old-world charm, solicitous staff and a reputation for excellent cuisine and service.

✉ Gran Via de les Corts Catalanes 668 ☎ 93 318 52 00; www.ritzbcn.com 🚇 Passeig de Gràcia

Omm (€€€)

The city's most fashionable hotel, with a rooftop plunge pool and Moo, a cutting-edge restaurant in the foyer. The monochrome rooms are cleverly designed to adapt to your needs, with movable storage space and light (both natural and artificial) that you manipulate to suit your mood.

✉ Carrer Rosselló 265 ☎ 93 445 40 00; www.hotelomm.es 🚇 Diagonal

RESTAURANTS

Alkimia (€€€)
See page 62.

Beltxenea (€€€)
Barcelona's premier Basque restaurant is set in an elegant 19th-century *Modernista* building, with a pretty interior garden terrace.
✉ Carrer Mallorca 275 ☎ 93 215 30 24 🕓 Closed Sat lunch, Sun
🚇 Diagonal, Passeig de Gràcia

Botafumeiro (€€€)
Fish is flown in daily from Galicia for this seafood restaurant. The *mariscos Botafumeira* (seafood platter) is a sight to behold.
✉ Carrer de Gran de Gràcia 81 ☎ 93 218 42 30 🕓 Daily 1pm–1am
🚇 Fontana

Casa Calvet (€€€)
See page 62.

Cinc Sentits (€€€)
See page 62.

La Dama (€€€)
See page 62.

Dragonfly (€€)
This stylish place evokes Old Shanghai, with sepia photographs and other oriental paraphernalia. Peking duck and steamboats form part of the menu.
✉ Carrer València 232 ☎ 93 451 11 28 🕓 Closed Sun pm 🚇 Diagonal, Passeig de Gràcia

Flash Flash (€€)
The genuine 1970s decor is a real draw to this popular eatery specializing in *tortillas* (omelettes – try the truffle omelette for something exotic) and truly great burgers.
✉ Carrer Granada de Penedès 25 ☎ 93 237 09 90 🕓 Daily 🚇 FGC Gràcia

Kresala (€€€)

Exquisite culinary delights served in striking surroundings of tangerine and pale-green ceramics, and enhanced by original art deco silverware.

✉ Carrer Santa Teresa 10 ☎ 93 218 30 30 🕐 Closed Sun, 3 weeks Aug
🚇 Diagonal

Mé (€€)

This unusual restaurant fuses Vietnamese and Creole cuisines into startling dishes such as 'firecracker' prawns. The soft jazz soundtrack and cocktail list give the place a cosy, bistro-type feel.

✉ Carrer Paris 162 ☎ 93 419 49 33 🕐 Dinner only; closed Sun 🚇 Diagonal

La Miafanera (€€)

This stylish eatery specializes in rice dishes from Asian 'sticky rices' to Italian risotto. Try the well-priced tasting menu, which lets you choose three rice dishes and comes with appetizers and finishes with an incredible salted chocolate dessert.

✉ Carrer Sagués 16 ☎ 93 240 59 12 🕐 Closed Sun, Mon 🚌 7, 33, 34

Le Relais de Venise (€€)

This classic French restaurant, seemingly unchanged since the 1950s, serves only entrecôte and pomme frites, but the quality and service make up for lack of choice. Leave room for dessert.

✉ Carrer Pau Claris 142 ☎ 93 467 21 62 🕐 Daily 🚇 Passeig de Gràcia

Toc (€€€)

This gourmet restaurant has been making waves in the city's food circles for its cuisine and interior design which mixes *Modernista* with contemporary, the work of local creative Jordi Torres.

✉ Carrer Girona 59 ☎ 93 488 11 48 🕐 Closed Sun 🚇 Girona

Tragaluz (€€)

A good place to tempt your taste buds with New Catalan Cuisine, which uses local ingredients in inventive ways. The name means 'skylight' and the place won a major design award when it opened.

✉ Pasaje de la Concepción 5 ☎ 93 487 01 96 🕐 Daily 🚇 Diagonal

CAFÉS AND *TAPAS* BARS

Cerveceria Catalana

See page 60.

La Bodegueta

An old wine tavern that is well known for its charcuterie and local wines.

✉ Rambla de Catalunya 100 ☎ 93 215 48 94 🕓 Closed Sun lunch 🚇 Provença

Pasteleria Mauri

Elegant, timeless pastry shop and café where high tea and coffee are served. A favourite with local residents and businesspeople. For something savoury, try the delicious finger sandwiches and croquettes.

✉ Rambla Catalunya 102 ☎ 93 215 10 20 🕓 Daily 🚇 Diagonal

SHOPPING

CLOTHES, JEWELLERY AND ACCESSORIES

Adolfo Domínguez

Adolfo Domínguez is one of Spain's most successful fashion designers, producing stylish, highly wearable clothing for men and women.

✉ Passeig de Gràcia 32 ☎ 93 487 41 70 🚇 Passeig de Gràcia

Bagués

Run by an old family of gold and silversmiths, this shop on the ground floor of Casa Amatller (➤ 134) contains priceless works by Masriera, the sole creator of the *Modernista* style in the Spanish jewellery trade.

✉ Passeig de Gràcia 41 ☎ 93 216 01 73 🚇 Passeig de Gràcia

Contribuciones y Moda

Large fashion outlet store for men and women selling last year's high-fashion labels at great prices. Upstairs has more everyday wear, from mainly Spanish brands.

✉ Carrer de Sant Miquel 30 ☎ 93 218 71 40 🚇 Diagonal

Desigual

The fresh and funky street and urban wear from this local label is known for bold, dramatic prints and quirky styling.

✉ Passeig de Gràcia 7 🚇 Passeig de Gràcia

Joaquín Berao

Jewellery by Joaquín Berao, celebrated for his unusual combinations of materials and avant-garde chunky designs.

✉ Rambla de Catalunya 74 ☎ 93 215 00 91 🚇 Diagonal

Loewe

See page 80.

Lydia Delgado

Delgado is one of Barcelona's most distinctive local designers of elegant, easy-to-wear women's fashions.

✉ Carrer Minerva 21 ☎ 93 415 99 98 🚇 Gràcia, Diagonal

Muxart Chic

This is a vibrant shop showcasing shoes by Barcelonan shoe designer, Muxart.

✉ Carrer Roselló 230 ☎ 93 488 10 64 🚇 Provença, Diagonal

Nobodinoz

For trendy kids, and their parents, this beautiful concept store sells designer clothing, toys and knick-knacks for the young ones.

✉ Carrer Séneca 9 ☎ 93 368 63 35 🚇 Diagonal

La Perla Gris

Lingerie and swimwear from all the best brands.

✉ Rambla Catalunya 112 ☎ 93 218 07 96 🚇 Diagonal

Regia

This is Barcelona's prime perfumery and it even has its own small 'Perfume Museum' at the back of the shop, which may be visited (moderate).

✉ Passeig de Gràcia 39 ☎ 93 216 01 21 🚇 Passeig de Gràcia

ARTS, CRAFTS, GIFTS AND DESIGN

Centre Català d'Artesania
See page 80.

Compagnie Française de l'Orient et de la Chine
Beautiful craft and clothing from the Far East is sold here, from
gorgeous ceramics and lacquerware to embroidered slippers and
coats and Chairman Mao kitsch. With wooden shop-fittings and
shelves, the shop evokes a colonial market place.
✉ Carrer Valencia 225 ☎ 93 215 48 83 🚇 Passeig de Gràcia

D Barcelona
A wide choice of gifts and avant-garde household items,
together with temporary exhibitions presenting the work
of talented young designers as well as some of the more
established names.
✉ Avinguda Diagonal 367 ☎ 93 216 03 46 🚇 Diagonal

Dom
Homeware, knick-knacks, gadgets and designer toys inspired by
the 1960s and 1970s are on sale in this intriguing shop. If it's a
beaded curtain or lava lamp you are after, look no further. Books
and magazines on art and design are also available.
✉ Carrer Provença 249 ☎ 93 342 55 91 🚇 Diagonal

Dos I Una
The first design shop in Barcelona – it is tiny, but it has a wealth of
gadgets and unusual gift ideas.
✉ Carrer Rosselló 275 ☎ 93 217 70 32 🚇 Diagonal

Puzzlemanía
As the name suggests, Puzzlemanía sells over a thousand different
types of jigsaw puzzle.
✉ Carrer Diputació 225 ☎ 93 451 58 03 🚇 Universitat

Vinçon
See page 81.

BOOKS, MUSIC AND ANTIQUES

Casa del Libre

Spain's answer to WH Smith with an enormous selection of books on all subjects and in most languages. Inside the front entrance, coffee-table books on Barcelona are sold, from monographs on Gaudí to Barcelona design tomes.

✉ Passeig de Gràcia 62 ☎ 93 272 34 80 🚇 Passeig de Gràcia

Laie

An eclectic collection of literature and books on art in a lovely shop with an upstairs café which often hosts book readings.

✉ Carrer Pau Claris 85 ☎ 93 318 17 39 🕔 Café: Tue–Fri 8:30am–1am, Sat 10am–1am, Mon 8:30am–9pm 🚇 Urquinaona

FOOD AND DRINK

Cacao Sampaka

This fabulous chocolate 'boutique' arranges its chocolate blocks and bon-bons into 'collections' such as spices, flowers and so on. You can pick and choose your own selection, or sample some of their goodies in the rear café.

✉ Carrer Consell de Cent 292 ☎ 93 272 08 33 🚇 Passeig de Gràcia

Colmado Quillez

Barcelona's most famous traditional grocery store, selling an array of tinned foods, preserves, cold meats and wines.

✉ Rambla de Catalunya 63 ☎ 93 215 23 56 🚇 Passeig de Gràcia

Murrià

This *Modernista* store first opened in 1898, and today sells a wide assortment of cheeses, cold meats and other delicacies.

✉ Carrer Roger de Llúria 85 ☎ 93 215 57 89 🚇 Passeig de Gràcia

Xampany

The only shop devoted solely to the sale of *cava* (sparkling wine). More than 100 varieties to choose from.

✉ Carrer València 200 ☎ 93 453 93 38 🚇 Passeig de Gràcia

ENTERTAINMENT

Dry Martini

Although it's been around only since the 1980s, this classic cocktail bar a evokes genuine speakeasy ambience with its leather sofas, wooden whiskey-lined shelves, low lighting and smooth jazz on the soundtrack. The cocktails, served by attentive white-aproned waiters, are top flight.

✉ Carrer Aribau 86 ☎ 93 217 50 72 🕐 Daily Ⓜ Diagonal

Luz de Gas

This *fin de siècle* music hall has been made over into one of Barcelona's classiest venues, with live music, from salsa to rock, most nights of the week followed by a DJ to the early hours. Dress up and be prepared to queue at the door at weekends.

✉ Carrer Muntaner 246 ☎ 93 209 77 11 🕐 Daily Ⓜ FGC Muntaner

Nick Havanna

This was one of Barcelona's original 'design bars' when it opened in the late 1980s. Although the decor has been trumped in other places, it remains a classic of the city's nightlife.

✉ Carrer Rosselló 208 ☎ 93 217 77 32 🕐 Thu–Sat midnight–6am
Ⓜ Diagonal

Otto Zutz

This is one of the most fashionable and liveliest clubs in town, and a *tour de force* of design, with its clever lighting and metal staircases and galleries. Dress smartly and arrive after midnight.

✉ Carrer Lincoln 15 ☎ 93 238 07 22 🕐 Wed–Sat midnight–5am
Ⓜ Fontana, Passeig de Gràcia

Montjuïc to Sants

Montjuïc, a steep mountain to the south of the city, once had a Roman settlement and temple to Jupiter crowning its heights. Since the 1929 International Exhibition, however, pretty pavilions have been converted to exhibition palaces, Olympic stadiums and concert halls.

One of the best ways to reach Montjuïc is by funicular railway, from the Avinguda Paral.lel Metro station. The Drassanes, the city's medieval shipyards which have been transformed into Barcelona's highly acclaimed Museu Marítim, lie to the east of Montjuïc at the port end of Las Ramblas, close to the station.

Once on Montjuïc, you'll find two of the city's greatest art museums, one dedicated to Joan Miró and his colourful works, the other showing a world-renowned collection of Catalan Romanesque frescoes that were rescued from decaying Pyrenean churches.

The Sants neighbourhood lies on the northern side of Montjuïc, and this is where you'll find Barcelona's main train station of the same name. At the foot of Montjuïc, on the eastern side, the residential neighbourhood of Poble Sec has some attractive houses and squares, and cosy cafés and bars, particularly along the Carrer de Blai.

L'ANELLA OLÍMPICA

In 1992, Montjuïc was temporarily renamed 'Mount Olympus' and became Barcelona's main venue for the Olympic Games. Atop its western crest lies the Anella Olímpica (Olympic Ring), a vast complex of concrete and marble that contains some of the city's most celebrated new buildings: Ricardo Bofills' neoclassical sports university; the Institut Nacional de Educació Fisica de Catalunya (INEFC); the Complex Esportiu Bernat Picornell swimming-pool complex; Santiago Calatrava's communications tower, which dominates the skyline; and the black steel and glass domed Palau de Sant Jordi, designed by Japanese architect Arata Isozaki, which looks more like a UFO than a covered sports stadium.

Barcelona had bid for the games three times previously and had built Europe's biggest stadium for the 1929 World Exhibition with the clear intention of using it for the 1936 'People's Olympics' (organized as an alternative to the infamous Berlin Games). These never took place due to the outbreak of Spanish Civil War the day before the official opening. For the 1992 games, local architects managed to preserve the stadium's original façade, while increasing the seating capacity from 25,000 to 70,000 by excavating deep into the interior. It is now mainly used for large-scale sporting and music events, though highlights of the 1992 games can be relived through video clippings and souvenir showcases in the **Galería Olímpica,** located beneath the stadium.

🚏 14K ✉ Avinguda de l'Estadi/Passeig Olímpic, Montjuïc ☎ Palau Sant Jordi: 93 426 20 89; Picornell swimming pools: 93 423 4041
✋ Free (except for events) 🚇 Espanya, or Paral.lel, then Funicular de Montjuïc 🚌 61
Galería Olímpica ☎ 93 292 53 79
🕐 Mon, Wed–Sat 10–6, Sun 10–2
✋ Moderate 🚌 50

FUNDACIÓ JOAN MIRÓ
Best places to see, ➤ 40–41.

MONTJUÏC
Best places to see, ➤ 42–43.

MUSEU NACIONAL D'ART DE CATALUNYA
Best places to see, ➤ 44–45.

PARC DE L'ESPANYA INDUSTRIAL

With works by many Catalan artists, this is Barcelona's most controversial park – a *nou urbanisme* project, built between 1982 and 1985 on the site of an old factory. It is built on two levels, the lower part comprising a large lake and grassy area, with steep white steps up to the much-scorned upper esplanade, where there are ten lighthouses, a series of water spouts and an immense metal play-sculpture entitled the *Dragon of St George*.

⊞ 15G ✉ Carrer de Rector Triado 🚇 Sants-Estació

PARC DE JOAN MIRÓ

This enduringly popular park occupies an entire city block on what was formerly the site of a massive abattoir, hence its nickname Parc de l'Escorxador (slaughterhouse). It was created in the 1980s, and is always full of people reading, jogging, dog-walking or playing *petanca* (boules)

amid the attractive pergolas and orderly rows of shady palm trees. The park's most famous feature, however, is a startling sculpture 22m (72ft) high by Joan Miró, covered in multicoloured ceramic fragments, named *Dona i Ocell* (Woman and Bird).

🕇 16G ✉ Carrer de Tarragona 🚇 Espanya 🚌 9, 13, 27, 30, 50, 56, 57, 65, 91, 109, 157

PAVELLÓ MIES VAN DER ROHE

Modernist architect Ludwig Mies van der Rohe created this masterpiece of modern 'international' design for the 1929 World Exhibition at Montjuïc, a construction of astonishing simplicity and finesse in marble, onyx, glass and chrome, widely acknowledged as one of the classic buildings of the 20th century. It was dismantled at the end of the fair and subsequently meticulously reconstructed and reopened (in its original location) in 1986, on the centenary of Mies van der Rohe's birth.

Inside, take time to enjoy the quality of the colours, textures and materials, as well as a striking bronze sculpture entitled *Der Morgen* (The Morning) and the famous 'Barcelona' chair, a design of timeless elegance created by Mies van der Rohe especially for the Expo, which has since been copied worldwide.

www.miesbcn.com

🕇 15J ✉ Avinguda del Marquès de Comillas s/n
☎ 93 423 40 16 🕓 Daily 10–8 💷 Moderate 🚇 Espanya 🚌 13, 50, 61 and all routes to Plaça Espanya

POBLE ESPANYOL

You can tour the whole of Spain in an afternoon here at Barcelona's 'Spanish Village', a remarkable showcase of regional architectural styles.

Built for the 1929 World Exhibition, the Poble Espanyol (Spanish Village) was intended as a re-creation of the diversity of Spanish regional architecture through the ages. The 115 life-sized reproductions of buildings, clustered around 6 squares and 3km (5 miles) of streets, form an authentic village, where visitors can identify famous or characteristic buildings ranging from the patios of Andalucia to Mallorcan mansions and the granite façades of Galicia.

Within the village are bars and restaurants serving regional specialities, and more than 60 shops selling folk crafts and regional artefacts. Some are undeniably over-priced, but there are also some real finds. The Fundació Fran Daural, located inside the 'village', boasts a few Dalís and Picassos and is definitely worth paying the extra, inexpensive entrance fee.

At night the Poble Espanyol takes on a different air with a handful of nightclubs and bars such as La Terraza (➤ 154) and El Tablao de Carmen (➤ 154) located inside its walls. During the summer during El Grec cultural festival, the main square acts a stage for concerts. In the past years Bob Dylan and Van Morrison have both played here.

www.poble-espanyol.com

🏠 15J 📧 Avinguda de Marqués de Comillas s/n
☎ 93 508 63 00 🕐 Mon 9am–8pm; Tue–Thu 9am–2am; Fri–Sat 9am–4am; Sun 9am–midnight 💵 Moderate
🍴 Plenty (€–€€) 🚇 Espanya 🚌 50

HOTEL

Hotel AC Miramar (€€€)

This luxury hotel is perched on the southern crest of Montjuïc and offers stunning views of the city and sea from its modern rooms.

✉ Plaça Carlos Ibáñez 3 ☎ 93 281 16 01; www.achotels.com 🚌 50

RESTAURANTS

Tapioles 53

See page 63.

Visual (€€€)

This haute cuisine restaurant on the 23rd floor of an office building near Sants station has staggering city views.

✉ Avinguda Roma 2–4 ☎ 93 600 69 96 🕐 Daily 🚇 Sants

Xemei (€€)

This pretty restaurant serves excellent Venetian food such as spaghetti with clams and rice cooked in squid ink.

✉ Passeig de l'Exposició 85 ☎ 93 553 51 40 🕐 Closed Tue and Wed
🚇 Poble Sec

SHOPPING

Elephant Book Store

Barcelona's only second-hand English-language bookstore with mountains of titles to dig through at bargain-basement prices.

✉ Carrer Creu de Molers 12 ☎ 93 443 05 94 🕐 Daily 🚇 Poble Sec

Poble Espanyol

More than 60 art and craft shops in a reproduction 'Spanish Village' (152) selling traditional wares from all corners of Spain.

✉ Avinguda del Marqués de Comillas s/n ☎ 93 508 63 00 🚌 13, 61
🚇 Espanya

ENTERTAINMENT

Mercat de les Flors

Innovative dance, drama and music in a converted flower market.

✉ Carrer Lleida 59 ☎ 93 426 18 75 🚇 Espanya

Space

This smaller version of the famous Ibizan club packs them in at weekends. Popular with a mainly young crowd of techno and house enthusiasts.

✉ Carrer Tarragona 141–147 ☎ 93 426 84 44 🕓 Fri–Sat midnight–6am
🚇 Tarragona

El Tablao de Carmen

Highly rated flamenco cabaret at the Poble Espanyol. Dinner is also available.

✉ Carrer Arcs 9, Poble Espanyol, Montjuïc ☎ 93 325 68 95
🕓 Tue–Sun 8pm–2am ❓ Shows Tue–Sun 9:30 and 11:30pm.
Reservations recommended

La Terrazza

Summertime open-air club takes place on Montjuïc, behind Poble Espanyol.

✉ Avinguda Marquès de Comilas, Montjuïc ☎ 93 272 49 80 🕓 Thu–Sat
midnight–6am 🚇 Espanya

Tinta Roja

Run by an Argentinian family, this spacious yet cosy bar decorated with red drapes and fading antiques is a great place to have a quiet drink and offers the occasional live show, from trapeze artists to tango.

✉ Carrer de la Creu dels Molers 17 ☎ 93 443 32 43 🕓 Wed–Sat 8pm–3am
🚇 Poble Sec

Up And Down

Barcelona's most adult nightclub. Upstairs, an affluent, black-tie crowd; contemporary club music downstairs.

✉ Carrer Numància 179 ☎ 93 205 51 94 🕓 Tue–Sun midnight–5:30am
🚇 Sants ❓ Men must wear a tie

TIBIDABO

PEDRALBES

Pedralbes and Tibidabo

The city's efficient public transport will whisk you to Barcelona's outlying districts and some of its top destinations.

In the western neighbourhood of Pedralbes sits the splendid royal monastery of the same name, the perfect place to escape the bustle of the city. South of the monastery, off the Avinguda Diagonal, lies the Palau Reial de Pedralbes, a royal palace that now houses a museum of ceramics and a museum of decorative arts.

The section of the Avinguda Diagonal that cuts through the district of Les Corts, between the Palau Reial de Pedralbes and Plaça de Francesc Macià, is lined with offices, banks and apartment buildings, though a mega-mall and classy shops make it a popular place for retail therapy.

To the south is FC Barcelona's stadium, Camp Nou, where football fans flock to see their team in action. To the north are Barcelona's ultramodern science museum, CosmoCaixa, and Tibidabo, where you can ride on roller-coasters with the whole city laid out spectacularly before you.

MONESTIR DE PEDRALBES

The monastery of Pedralbes was founded by King Jaume II and Queen Elisenda de Montcada in 1326 to accommodate nuns of the St Clare of Assisi order. Following the king's death in 1327, Elisenda spent the last 37 years of her life here.

The spacious, three-storey cloisters are one of the architectural jewels of Barcelona. Step inside and it is hard to believe you are just a short bus ride from downtown Barcelona. From here, there is access to the refectory, the chapter house and the queen's grave. St Michael's Chapel is one of the highlights of a visit. It is decorated with remarkable murals by Spanish painter Ferrer Bassa depicting Christ's Passion and the life of the Virgin Mary.

Monastic life in the 14th century is illustrated through permanent exhibitions in the original refectory, with its vaulted ceiling, the infirmary and the kitchens. Next door in the Gothic church you can hear nuns of the founding order sing during Mass.

🚌 2A ✉ Baixada de Monestir 9 ☎ 93 256 34 34 🕓 Monastery: Tue–Sun 10–2. Church: Tue–Sun 11–2, 6:30–8. Daily Mass at 7pm ✋ Moderate
🚌 22, 63, 64, 75 ❓ Bookshop, gift shop

MUSEU DEL FUTBOL CLUB BARCELONA

If you can't get a ticket to see one of Europe's top football teams in action, then at least visit the Barcelona Football Club Museum, the city's most visited museum after the Picasso Museum (► 46–47). Even those who loathe football can't help marvelling at the vast Camp Nou stadium, which seats more than 98,000 spectators. The museum, under the terraces, presents a triumphant array of trophies, photographs and replays of highlights

in the club's history before leading you to the shop, where everyone can buy that essential club shirt, scarf, badge…

FC Barcelona, or Barça for short, is more than a football club. During the Franco era, it stood as a Catalan symbol around which people could rally, and this emotional identification still remains today. It also explains why this legendary club has the world's largest soccer club membership (more than 140,000 members) and why the streets still erupt with ecstatic revellers following a win over arch-rivals, Real Madrid.

www.fcbarcelona.com

🚌 1D ✉ Camp Nou – Entrance 7 or 9, Carrer Arístides Maillol
☎ 93 496 36 00 🕓 Mon–Sat 10–8, Sun 10–2:30 ✋ Moderate 🍴 Café (€)
Ⓜ Collblanc, Maria Cristina ❓ Gift shop

PALAU REIAL DE PEDRALBES

The Royal Palace of Pedralbes accommodated the Spanish Royal family during the International Exhibition of 1929. After 1939 it was used by Franco and then royalty and heads of state, before being opened to the public in 1960, along with the stately gardens. Today the state rooms house two museums. The Museu de Ceràmica traces the development of Spanish ceramics from the 12th century onwards, and includes the 18th-century Catalan panels *La Cursa de Braus* (the Bullfight) and *La Xocolotada* (The Chocolate Party), together with works by Picasso and Miró. The Museu de les Arts Decoratives has an impressive collection of decorative arts from the early Middle Ages to the present day. Special emphasis is placed on 20th-century developments, from *Modernisme* to Functionalism and Minimalism.

www.museuartsdecoratives.com

✚ 2C ✉ Avinguda de la Diagonal 686 ☎ 93 280 50 24 🕓 Museums: Tue–Sat 10–5, Sun 10–3. Park: open until dusk ✋ Museums: moderate, free 1st Sun of month 🚇 Palau Reial 🚌 7, 33, 67, 68, 74, 75 ❓ Shop, library

TIBIDABO AND SERRA DE COLLSEROLA

Mont Tibidabo, 550m (1,800ft) high, forms the northwestern boundary of Barcelona and has panoramic views over the entire city, and, on exceptionally clear days, of Mallorca. The best views are from the **Torre de Collserola,** a telecommunications tower with a lookout point. At its summit, and topped by a huge statue of Christ, stands the modern Church of the Sacred Heart (Sagrat Cor). Nearby, the **Parc d'Atraccions** (➤ 69) cleverly balances traditional rides with high-tech attractions on several levels of the mountaintop, and is a fun day out for the family. Tibidabo is just one of the mountains of the Collserola range, a wonderful 6,550ha (16,200 arces) nature reserve with woodlands full of wildlife. It is best reached by FGC train to Baixador de Vallvidrera. From here, it is a 10-minute walk uphill to the **information centre,** where details of walks and cycles are available.

✚ 7A (off map)

Tibidabo Amusement Park

✉ Plaça Tibidabo 3–4 ☎ 93 221 79 42; www.tibidabo.es ⏰ Jul–Aug Wed–Sun noon–11. Check website for other dates 💶 Expensive 🚇 FGC Avinguda Tibidabo, then Tramvia Blau to Peu Funicular, then funicular

Torre de Collserola

✉ Carretera de Vallvidrera al Tibidabo s/n ☎ 93 406 93 54; www.torredecollserola.com ⏰ Jul–Aug Mon–Fri 11–2:30, 3:30–8, Sat–Sun 11–8; Apr–Jun, Sep Wed–Fri 11–2:30, 3:30–7, Sat–Sun 11–7; Oct–Mar closes 2 hours earlier 💶 Moderate 🚇 FGC Peu Funicular, then funicular

Collserola Information Centre

✉ Carretera de Vallvidrera a Sant Cugat, al km 4.7 ☎ 93 280 35 52 ⏰ Daily 9:30–3 🚇 FGC Baixador de Vallvidrera, then 10-minute walk

HOTEL

Gran Hotel La Florida (€€€)

Located 500m (1,640ft) above the city it has superb views and luxurious accommodation. There is original art work in the public spaces and an L-shaped lap pool on a superb terrace.

✉ Carretera de Vallvidrera al Tibidabo 83–93 ☎ 93 259 30 00; www.hotellaflorida.com

RESTAURANTS

Fragments (€)

This charming café on the prettiest square in Les Corts offers excellent *tapas* in the front room and more substantial meals in the dining room and garden. The *patatas bravas* are memorable, and it serves a great value *menu del día*.

✉ Plaça de la Concòrdia 12 ☎ 93 419 96 13 🕓 Closed Mon, Tue
🚇 Les Corts

Neichel (€€€)

This stylish restaurant boasts the talents of Alsace-born chef Jean-Louis Neichel, who has been described as 'the most brilliant ambassador French cuisine has ever had within Spain'.

✉ Carrer Beltrán í Rózpide 1–5 ☎ 93 203 84 08 🕓 Closed Sun, Mon, and 3 weeks in Aug 🚇 Maria Cristina

ENTERTAINMENT

Bikini

One of Barcelona's best nightspots, with a club playing rock/disco, a Latin-American salsa room and a classy cocktail lounge.

✉ Carrer Deu i Mata 105 ☎ 93 322 00 05 🕓 Wed–Sun midnight–5am
🚇 Les Corts

Danzatoria

With its restaurant, disco, terrace café and rambling gardens on the slopes of Tibidabo, this sophisticated place is a favourite summer venue, despite the lengthy uphill trek from the station.

✉ Avinguda Tibidabo 61 ☎ 93 221 62 61 🕓 Daily 10pm–3am 🚇 FGC Avinguda Tibidabo

Elephant

Glamorous bar-club decorated in the style of a Persian palace.

✉ Passeig dels Til·lers 1 ☎ 93 334 02 58 🕐 Wed–Sat 11:30pm–4am
Ⓜ Palau Reial

Renoir Les Corts

Excellent *multi sala* (multi-screen) cinema where all titles are shown in VO (original version) with Spanish subtitles. Mondays are discount entry nights and there are midnight screenings at weekends. There is a second branch near Sant Antoni Market (Carrer Floridablanca 135; Metro: Sant Antoni). For a full schedule, check out their website.

✉ Carrer Eugeni d'Ors 12 ☎ 93 490 55 10; www.cinesrenoir.com
Ⓜ Les Corts

Sala BeCool

Live indie music and a late-night club that pulls in, as the name says, a cool crowd.

✉ Plaça Joan Llongueras 5 ☎ 93 362 04 13; www.salabecool.com
🕐 Club sessions: Thu–Sat midnight–3am. Live gigs generally start 9–10pm
Ⓜ FGC Muntaner

SPORT

FOOTBALL
Camp Nou – FC Barcelona

No visit to Barcelona is complete without a visit to Camp Nou, Europe's largest stadium (seating 98,000), and its museum (➤ 157).

✉ Avinguda Aristides Maillol. Museum: Gate 7 or 9 ☎ 93 496 36 00
Ⓜ Collblanc, Maria Cristina

TENNIS
Vall Parc Club

Fourteen open-air tennis courts on Tibidabo. Racquets (not balls) for hire.

✉ Carretera de l'Arrabassada s/n ☎ 93 212 67 89; www.vallparc.com
🚌 119

Excursions

It would be a shame to visit Barcelona without also seeing something of Catalunya (Catalonia). Despite being an autonomous province of Spain, this region feels in many ways like a separate country, with its own language and traditions, culture and cuisine. Its geographical location makes it the gateway to Spain. Over time the passage of many peoples and civilizations has shaped the region, leaving cities such as Girona and Tarragona brimming with historical monuments, while its beautiful landscapes have provided inspiration for such artists as Gaudí, Miró, Dalí and Picasso.

The Catalan landscape is easy to tour and offers a wide variety of scenery, from the dramatic, snow-capped peaks of the Pyrenees and the secret bays and bustling fishing ports of the Costa Brava, north of Barcelona, to the acclaimed Penedès vineyards and long golden beaches of the Costa Daurada to the south.

FIGUERES

The main claim to fame of Figueres, two hours' drive northwest of Barcelona and 17km (10.5 miles) from the Franco-Spanish border, is that the great Surrealist painter Salvador Dalí was born here in 1904 and gave his first exhibition here when he was just 14. In 1974, he inaugurated his **Teatre-Museu Dalí,** in the old municipal theatre, and it remains one of Spain's most visited museums. It is the only museum in Europe dedicated exclusively to his works.

The building, topped with a massive metallic dome and decorated with egg shapes, is original and spectacular – in keeping with Dalí's powerful personality. Its galleries are housed in a number of enclosed, circular tiers around a central stage and a courtyard containing a 'Rainy Cadillac' and a tower of car tyres crowned by a boat and an umbrella. The galleries contain paintings, sculptures, jewellery, drawings and other works from his private collection along with weird and wonderful constructions from different periods of his career, including a bed with fish tails, skeletal figures and even a complete life-sized orchestra. Dalí died in Figueres in 1989, leaving his entire estate to the Spanish State. His body lies behind a simple granite slab inside the museum.

🚹 Plaça del Sol ☎ 972 50 31 55 🍴 Plenty (€–€€)

Teatre-Museu Dalí

✉ Plaça Gala-Salvador Dalí 5 ☎ 972 67 75 00 🕐 Jul–Sep daily 9–8; Oct, Mar–Jun Tue–Sun 9:30–6; Nov–Feb Tue–Sun 10:30–6. Closed 1 Jan, 25 Dec 💷 Expensive ❓ Last ticket sold 45 minutes before closing

GIRONA

Just 1.5 hours by car or train from Barcelona, the beautiful, walled city of Girona is one of Catalonia's most characterful cities, with an admirable collection of ancient monuments. The old city, built on a steep hill and known for its lovely stairways, arcaded streets and sunless alleys, is separated from modern Girona by the River Onyar. The medieval, multicoloured houses overhanging the river are a photographer's dream, especially when seen from the iron footbridge designed by Eiffel. Most of the main sights are in the old city. Make sure you also allow time to shop along the beautiful Rambla de la Llibertat and to enjoy a drink in the arcaded Plaça de la Independencia.

At the heart of the old city, centred around Carrer de la Força, El Call, the old Jewish quarter, is one of the best preserved in western Europe and is particularly atmospheric by night, with its street lanterns and intimate restaurants. Another splendid sight is the **Catedral,** with its impressive staircase leading up to a fine baroque façade, a magnificent medieval interior and the widest Gothic vault in Europe. Housed inside a monastery, the **Museu Arqueològic** (Archaeological Musuem) outlines the city's history, and provides access to the Passeig Arqueològic, a panoramic walk around the walls of the old city. Nearby, the 12th-century **Banys Arabs** (Arab Bath-house), probably designed by Moorish craftsmen following the Moors' occupation of Girona, is the best preserved of its kind in Spain after the Alhambra, particularly striking for its fusion of Arab and Romanesque styles.

 Rambla de la Llibertat 1 ☎ 972 22 65 75 🍴 Plenty (€–€€)

Catedral

✉ Plaça de la Catedral ☎ 972 21 44 26 🕐 Daily 10–6:30 ✋ Moderate; free Sat pm and Sun

Museu Arqueològic

✉ Monestir Sant Pere de Galligans ☎ 972 20 26 32 🕐 Jun–Sep Tue–Sat 10:30–1:30, 4–7, Sun 10–2; Oct–May Tue–Sat 10–2, 4–6, Sun 10–2 ✋ Inexpensive

Banys Arabs

✉ Carrer Ferran Catolic ☎ 972 19 07 97 🕐 Apr–Sep Mon–Sat 10–7, Sun 10–2; Oct–Mar daily 10–2 ✋ Inexpensive

MONTSERRAT

Catalonia's holy mountain is 56km (35 miles) northwest of Barcelona with a summit of 1,200m (3,937ft). Montserrat is named after its strangely serrated rock formations (*mont*, mountain; *serrat*, sawed) and is one of the most important pilgrimage sites in the whole of Spain. Thousands travel here every year to venerate a medieval statue of the Madonna and Child called La Moreneta (The Black Virgin), blackened by the smoke of millions of candles over the centuries. The statue is said to have been made by St Luke and brought to the area by St Peter, and is displayed above the altar of the monastery church.

The spectacularly located monastery, founded in 1025, is also famous for its choir, *La Escolania*, one of the oldest and best-known boys' choirs in Europe, dating from the 13th century. The choir sings daily in the **Basilica,** a striking edifice containing important paintings including works by El Greco and Caravaggio.

Montserrat is clearly signposted by road from Barcelona, although the most enjoyable way to get there is by FGC train from Plaça d'Espanya, followed by a thrilling cable-car ride up to the monastery.

🏛 Plaça de la Creu, Montserrat ☎ 93 877 77 77 🍴 Limited choice of bars and restaurants

Basilica

✉ Monestir de Montserrat 🕐 Daily 8–6:30. La Escolania performs Mon–Fri at 1pm, Mon–Thu at 6:45pm and Sun at noon

EL PENEDÈS

Just an hour by train from Barcelona, El Penedès is Catalonia's wine country, perhaps not as well known outside Spain as La Rioja but producing some excellent wines all the same. Many *bodegas* (wineries) are open to the public (➤ 172). But even if you are not particularly interested in viniculture, El Penedès is a glorious place to visit, with its valleys of vineyards, pretty medieval villages and proximity to Montserrat (➤ 169), Catalonia's 'sacred mountain'.

The capital of the region is the bustling Vilafranca, a handsome town with some pretty *Modernista* architecture and arcaded streets in the old quarter. In the Gothic quarter, surrounded by squares, palaces and churches, the **Museu del Vi** is the only museum in Catalonia to be wholly dedicated to wine. Current methods of production can be observed at Vilafranca's three top wineries – **Mas Tinell, Jean León** and **Miguel Torres** – all outside the town centre (ask at the tourist office (➤ 172) for details. Every

Saturday morning a produce market is held in Plaça de la Vila in front of the Gothic *ajuntament* (town hall). Farmers come from all over the region to set up stalls, and it's a great place to pick up olives, charcuterie, cheeses and other local delicacies. While you are here, visit the Basílica de Santa Maria in the adjacent Plaça Sant Jaume (contact tourist office for opening hours), a 15th-century Gothic church and climb the 52m (170ft) bell tower for a great view of Vilafranca's interesting skyline. Vilafranca is famous for its *castellers* (human towers that perform during the city's main festa, held during the last week of August) and opposite the church a monument has been erected in their honour. Off and around the square the narrow streets are full of good bars, serving local wines and dishes such as *xató*, an endive and cod salad served with a delicious sauce of nuts, olive oil and dried peppers.

The villages around Vilafranca are definitely worth exploring. Sant Martí Sarroca contains an important Romanesque church with a splendid Gothic altarpiece and a 9th-century castle. Sant Sadorní d'Anoia is where most of El Penedès' *cava* (local sparkling wine) is produced with

66 *cava* firms dotted throughout the town. The largest, Codornìu, produces around 40 million bottles a year and its magnificent *Modernista* plant is open to visitors daily. Tours last 90 minutes and include a tasting. In Freixenet, the village's most emblematic *bodega*, built in *Modernista* style, is located right next to its railway station. In Torrelles de Foix, panoramic views of the entire area can be had from the Sanctuario de la Virgen de Foix, an ancient church built in honour of the region's patron saint. The village is also famous for Fuentes de les Dous, 35 natural springs that form a pretty waterfall.

The best time to visit El Penedès is in September during harvest when the vineyards are a hive of activity. Many villages also hold *verema* festivals, when the first wines of the season are drunk, usually in early October. Dates vary so check at the tourist office for details.

Vilafranca de Penedès Tourist Office

✉ Carrer Cort 14 ☎ 93 892 03 58

Museu del Vi

www.museudelvi.org

✉ Plaça Jaume I, 1 and 3, Vilafranca del Penedès
☎ 93 890 05 82 🕓 Jun–Aug Tue–Sat 10–7, Sun 10–2; Sep–May Tue–Sat 10–2, 4–7, Sun 10–2 ✋ Inexpensive

Penedès Wineries

☎ Codorníu: 93 891 33 42; Jean León: 93 899 55 12; Mas Tinell: 93 817 05 86; Miguel Torres: 93 817 73 30
🕓 Opening times vary. Contact individual wineries for details

SITGES

Sitges, 40km (25 miles) south of Barcelona, is one of Spain's oldest bathing resorts and has long been the weekend and holiday playground of Barcelonans. It was once a sleepy fishing port and, although it has now developed into a thriving seaside destination, the old town still retains its ancient charm, with narrow streets, whitewashed cottages and flower-festooned balconies. It also has several appealing *Modernista* buildings.

It was artist and writer Santiago Rusinyol who first put Sitges on the map, bringing it to the attention of artists such as Manuel de Falla, Ramon Casas, Nonell, Utrillo and Picasso. Rusinyol's house, **Cau Ferrat,** is today a museum, containing works by El Greco and Picasso among others. Neighbouring **Museu Maricel de Mar** houses an interesting collection of medieval and baroque artefacts, and the nearby **Museu Romántic** provides a fascinating insight into 18th-century patrician life in Sitges.

Sitges is famous for its beautiful Platja d'Or (Golden Beach), which stretches southwards for 5km (3 miles) from the baroque church of Sant Bartomeu i Santa Tecla. Its palm-fringed promenade is dotted with beach bars, cafés and fish restaurants. However, the resort is perhaps best known for its vibrant nightlife, drawing a young cosmopolitan crowd throughout the summer season. It is also a popular gay holiday destination. From October to May, Sitges is considerably quieter, except during *Carnaval* in mid-February when the town once more comes alive with wild parties and showy parades, drawing spectators from afar.

🛈 Carrer Sinia Morera 1 ☎ 93 894 42 51 🍴 Plenty (€–€€)

Museums

✉ Cau Ferrat and Maricel de Mar: Carrer Fonolar; Romántic: Casa Llopis, Carrer Sant Gaudenci 1 ☎ Cau Ferrat and Maricel de Mar: 93 894 03 64; Romántic: 93 894 29 69 🕐 Jul–Sep Tue–Sat 9:30–2, 4–7, Sun 10–3; Oct–Jun Tue–Sat 9:30–2, 3:30–6:30, Sun 10–3 ✋ Cau Ferrat: moderate. Maricel de Mar and Romántic: inexpensive. Combined ticket available for all three museums ❓ Guided visits only, on the hour

TARRAGONA

This agreeable city is not very well known to most foreign visitors to the region, even though it contains the largest example of Roman remains in Spain, the remarkable architectural legacy of Roman Tarraco and was once capital of an area that covered half the Iberian peninsula. Originally settled by Iberians and then Carthaginians, it later became the base for the Roman conquest of Spain and the main commercial centre on this stretch of the coast until Barcelona and Valencia overshadowed it, after the Christian reconquest of Spain in the early 12th century.

The town is situated on a rocky hill, sloping down to the sea. The ancient upper town contains most of the Roman ruins, some interesting museums and an attractive medieval quarter with a grand cathedral. Below the Old Town lies the modern shopping district, centred on the Rambla Nova with its smart boutiques and restaurants, and a daily fruit and vegetable market in Plaça Corsini. Below the main town, the chief attraction of the lower part of the

city is the maritime district of El Serrallo with its colourful fishing fleet, traditional *Lonja* (fish auction), and dockside restaurants. The rocky coastline beyond conceals a couple of beaches, notably Platja Arrabassada and Platja Llarga.

In the hillside overlooking the sea, the **Amfiteatre Romà** (Roman Amphitheatre) was where the Romans held their public spectacles, including combats between gladiators and wild animals before an audience of 12,000 people. During the 12th century the

Romanesque church of Santa Maria del Miracle was built on the site, giving the beach below its name – El Miracle. Tarragona's grandiose **Catedral** – a magnificent Romanesque-Gothic building – was built as the centrepiece of the *ciutat antigua* (old city).

The fascinating **Museu Arqueològic** (Archaeological Museum) includes a section of the old Roman wall, statues of emperors, several sarcophagi and some interesting mosaics. Nearby stands

the Praetorium and the vaults of the first-century Roman Circus. The Praetorium is the site of the **Museu d'Història** (Tarragona History Museum), which traces the origins and history of the city through such treasures as the sarcophagus of Hipolitus, a masterpiece that was rescued from the sea in 1948.

Tarragona's most treasured Roman remains are housed in the **Museu i Necropolia Paleocristians** (Paleo-Christian Museum), in what was once an ancient necropolis, a 20-minute walk west of the city centre. It includes a valuable collection of mosaics, pottery, metalwork, glass and ivory. Currently closed for restoration.

For an overview of the old city and the hinterland of the Camp de Tarragona, walk the Passeig Arqueològic. This promenade encircles the northernmost half of the old town, around the Roman walls, of which 1km (0.5 miles) of the original 4km (2.5 miles) remains. Seven defence towers and gates still stand.

🚹 Carrer Major ☎ 977 24 52 03 🍴 Plenty (€–€€) ❓ You can visit the Amfiteatre, Passeig Arqueològic, Museu d'Història, Circ Romà and Casa Museu de Castellarnau on a combined ticket

Amfiteatre Romà
✉ Carrer Oleguer ☎ 977 24 25 79 🕓 Apr–Sep Tue–Sat 9–9, Sun 9–3; Oct–Mar Tue–Sat 9–3, Sun 10–3 ✋ Free

Catedral
✉ Plaça de la Seu ☎ 977 23 86 85 🕓 Summer Mon–Sat 10–1, 4–7; winter Mon–Sat 10–2

Museu Arqueològic
✉ Plaça del Rei 5 ☎ 977 23 62 09 🕓 Jun–Sep Tue–Sat 9:30–8:30, Sun 10–2; Oct–May Tue–Sat 9:30–1:30, 3:30–7, Sun 10–2 ✋ Moderate

Museu de Història
✉ Plaça del Rei ☎ 977 24 27 52 🕓 Apr–Sep Mon–Sat 9–9, Sun 9–3; Oct–Mar Mon–Sat 9–7, Sun 10–3 ✋ Moderate

Museu i Necropolia Paleocristians
✉ Passeig de la Independència s/n ☎ 977 21 11 75 🕓 Currently closed for restoration. Check at tourist office

HOTELS

FIGUERES
Hotel Durán (€)
This popular hotel also has a highly regarded restaurant that serves hearty traditional cuisine with a modern touch. It was a favourite haunt of Salvador Dalí and friends.
✉ Carrer Lasuaca 5 ☎ 972 50 12 50; www.hotelduran.com

GIRONA
Bellmirall (€)
Housed inside the ancient buildings of the Jewish quarter and near to the cathedral, this hotel feels more like a country dwelling – and it serves huge breakfasts to keep you going through the day.
✉ Carrer Bellmirall 3 ☎ 972 20 40 09; www.grn.es

Carlemany (€€€)
Stylish, modern hotel between the station and the old town has 90 rooms, and lots of modern art. Its restaurant is one of the best in town.
✉ Plaça Miquel Santaló ☎ 972 21 12 12; www.carlemany.es

MONTSERRAT
Abat Cisneros (€–€€)
The name of this 3-star hotel, set in Montserrat's main square, is derived from a title given to the head of Benedictine monasteries during the Middle Ages. The rooms in the hotel are near the monastery and there are also rooms in the former monks' cells.
✉ Plaça de Monestir, 08199 Montserrat ☎ 93 877 77 01; www.montserratvisita.com

SITGES
Celimar (€–€€)
This tastefully renovated 3-star *Modernista* hotel, with 26 rooms, is near the beach. Ask for a room with a balcony.
✉ Passeig de Ribera 20 ☎ 93 811 01 70; www.hotelcelimar.com

El Xalet (€)

El Xalet is a discreet hotel in a beautiful *Modernista* villa, with just 10 well-furnished rooms. Other facilities include a restaurant, pool and garden.

✉ Carrer Isla de Cuba 35 ☎ 93 811 0070; www.elxalet.com

TARRAGONA
Fòrum (€)

This hotel offers simple, clean rooms overlooking Plaça de la Font in the Old Town. It is situated above a jolly *bodega*-style restaurant.

✉ Plaça de la Font 37 ☎ 977 23 17 18

Imperial Tarraco (€€)

The Imperial Tarraco is currently Tarragona's top hotel (4-star). It is centrally situated overlooking both the sea and the Amfiteatre Romà (➤ 176).

✉ Passeig de Palmeres ☎ 977 23 30 40; www.husa.es

Urbis (€)

You'll find this reasonably priced, modern and comfortable 3-star hotel in the town centre, just off the Rambla Nova and near the daily fruit market.

✉ Plaça Corsini 10 ☎ 977 24 01 16; www.hotelurbiscentre.com

RESTAURANTS

GIRONA
Le Bistrot (€–€€)

Halfway up a medieval flight of stairs, this restaurant serves a selection of light snacks and also some more substantial French-inspired meals.

✉ Pujada Sant Domènic 4 ☎ 972 21 88 03

El Pou de Call (€€)

Local cuisine in traditional surroundings. Excellent-value *menú del diá* and wine list.

✉ Carrer de la Força 14 ☎ 972 22 37 74 ◷ Closed Sun pm

MONTSERRAT
Abat Cisneros (€€)
Montserrat's top restaurant. The 16th-century stone dining room used to contain the monastery stables.

✉ Hotel Abat Cisneros ☎ 93 877 77 01

SITGES
Mare Nostrum (€€)
Smart waterfront restaurant. Try the *Xato de Sitges* (grilled fish with a local variant of *romesco* sauce), or monkfish and prawns with garlic mousseline.

✉ Passeig de la Ribera 60–62 ☎ 93 894 33 93 🕐 Closed Wed and mid-Dec to end Jan

TARRAGONA
Bodega Celler Gras (€)
A good place to join the locals for *tapas* – pâtés, cheeses and charcuterie, including spicy *xoriço* and Mallorquin *sobrassada*.

✉ Carrer Governadir Gonzalez 8 ☎ 977 23 48 20 🕐 Closed Sun pm

Estació Maritima (€€€)
This is one of the best of the many fish restaurants and *tapas* bars that line the waterfront in the fishermen's district of Serralló.

✉ Moll de Costa Tinglade 4 ☎ 977 22 74 18 🕐 Closed Sun pm, Mon

Sol-Ric (€€)
Excellent fish restaurant located on the outskirts of town near Platja Rembassada.

✉ Via Augusta 227 ☎ 977 23 20 32 🕐 Closed Sun, Mon pm

VILAFRANCA DEL PENEDÈS
Cal Ton (€€€)
It may come as a surprise to find such a chic, gourmet restaurant in an otherwise traditional town. Try the mouth-watering pancakes filled with a seafood and *cava* sauce.

✉ Carrer del Casal 8 ☎ 93 890 37 41 🕐 Closed Sun pm, Mon, Easter week, 2 Aug

Sight Locator Index

This index relates to the maps on the covers. We have given map references to the main sights in the book. Some sights may not be plotted on the maps.

Index

Acknowledgements

The Automobile Association would like to thank the following photographers, companies and picture libraries for their assistance in the preparation of this book.

Abbreviations for the picture credits are as follows – (t) top; (b) bottom; (l) left; (r) right; (AA) AA World Travel Library.

4l Park Güell, AA/M Jourdan; **4c** Metro, AA/S L Day; **4r** Sagrada Família, AA/P Wilson; **5l** Las Ramblas, AA/P Enticknap; **5c** Museu d'Història de la Ciutat, AA/S L Day; **5r** Girona, AA/M Chaplow; **6/7** Park Güell, AA/M Jourdan; **8/9** Sagrada Família, AA/M Chaplow; **10/1t** Casa Milà, AA/S L Day; **10l** Barceloneta, AA/M Jourdan; **10r** Musician, AA/M Jourdan; **11c** Barri Gòtic, AA S L Day; **11b** Sagrada Família, AA/M Jourdan; **12/3** Mercat de la Boqueria, AA/M Jourdan; **12l** Olive oil, AA/S McBride; **12r** Mercat de Santa Caterina, AA/S McBride; **13** El Lobito restaurant, AA/S McBride; **14t** Casa Antigua, AA/M Chaplow; **14l** Meal, Restaurant Salamanca, AA/S McBride; **15tl** Gràcia market, AA/M Jourdan; **15cl** Wine shop, AA/S McBride; **15r** Wine bottles, AA/S McBride; **16** *Sardana* dancers, AA/S L Day; **17** Park Güell, AA/M Jourdan; **18** Plaça de Olles, AA/M Chaplow; **19t** Flamenco dancer, AA/M Jourdan; **19b** Mercat de la Boqueria, AA/S McBride; **20/1** Metro, AA/S L Day; **25** La Mercè, AA/M Jourdan; **27** Metro sign, AA/M Jourdan; **28** Taxi, Port Olímpic, AA/S L Day; **31** Public telephone, AA/P Wilson; **34/5** Sagrada Família, AA/P Wilson; **36/7** Casa Milà, AA/S L Day;

36 Casa Milà, AA/M Chaplow; **38** Cathedral, AA/ M Chaplow; **38/9** Cathedral, AA/S L Day; **39** Cathedral, AA/M Jourdan; **40/1** Fundació Joan Miró, AA/S L Day; **42/3** View from Castle Montjuïc, AA/M Jourdan; **43t** Montjuïc, AA/M Jourdan; **43b** Plaça de la Font Magica, AA/M Jourdan; **44** Museu Nacional d'Art de Catalunya, AA/M Jourdan; **44/5** Museu Nacional d'Art de Catalunya, AA/M Jourdan; **45** Museu Nacional d'Art de Catalunya, AA/M Jourdan; **46cl** Museu Picasso, AA/M Chaplow; **46bl** Museu Picasso, AA/P Wilson; **47** Museu Picasso, AA/M Chaplow; **48r** Park Güell, AA/S L Day; **48/9** Park Güell, AA/M Jourdan; **49** Park Güell, AA/M Jourdan; **50bl** Las Ramblas, AA/S L Day; **50br** Las Ramblas, AA/S L Day; **51** Las Ramblas, AA/M Chaplow; **52t** Passion Façade, Sagrada Família, AA/M Jourdan; **52/3** Sagrada Família, AA/M Jourdan; **53** Sagrada Família, AA/P Wilson; **54** Santa Maria del Mar, AA/M Jourdan; **54/5** Santa Maria del Mar, AA/M Jourdan; **55** Santa Maria del Mar, AA/P Wilson; **56/7** Cafés, Las Ramblas, AA/P Enticknap; **58** Café scene, AA/S L Day; **60/1** *Tapas* selection, AA/M Chaplow; **62/3** Restaurant interior, AA/S McBride; **64/5** View toward Plaça d'Espanya, AA/S L Day; **66/7** Mercat de la Boqueria, AA/S McBride; **69** L'Aquarium, AA/M Jourdan; **70/1** Golondrina, AA/M Jourdan; **72** Ajuntament, AA/S L Day; **72/3** Carrer del Bisbe, AA/S L Day; **75** Parc del Laberint, AA/M Chaplow; **76/7** Casa Milà, AA/S L Day; **78** Barcelona Head, AA/M Chaplow; **78/9** Dona i Ocell, AA/M Jourdan; **80/1** Shopping bag, AA/M Chaplow; **82/3** Museu Museu d'Història de la Ciutat, AA/M Jourdan; **85** Las Ramblas, AA/M Jourdan; **86/7** Plaça de Olles, AA/M Chaplow; **88** Musicians, AA/M Jourdan; **88/9** Drassanes and Museu Marítim, AA/M Jourdan; **90** Mercat de la Boqueria, AA/S McBride; **90/1** Columbus Monument, AA/S L Day; **92/3b** Museu d'Art Contemporani de Barcelona, AA/M Jourdan; **92/3c** Museu Frederic Marès, AA/S L Day; **94** Museu d'Història de la Ciutat, AA/M Jourdan; **95** Palau Güell, AA/M Jourdan; **96/7** Plaça de Catalunya, AA/S L Day; **97** Plaça del Rei, AA/M Jourdan; **98** Plaça Reial, AA/S L Day; **98/9** Plaça Reial, AA/P Wilson; Palau de la Generalitat, AA/S L Day; **100** Maremagnum, AA/M Jourdan; **113** La Ribera, AA/M Chaplow; **114/5** Arts Hotel, Port Olímpic, AA/M Chaplow; **115** Arts Hotel, Torre Mapfre, Port Olímpic, AA/M Chaplow; **117** Palau de Mar, AA/M Jourdan; **116/7** Palau de la Mar, AA/M Chaplow; **119** Palau de la Musica Catalana, AA/M Jourdan; **120** Parc de la Ciutadella, AA/S L Day; **127** Passeig de Gràcia, AA/M Chaplow;

128/9 L'Eixample, AA/M Chaplow; **129** Farmacia Bolos, AA/M Chaplow; **130/1** Fundació Antoni Tàpies, AA/M Jourdan; **131t** Casa Vicens, AA/M Jourdan; **131b** Casa Vicens, AA/M Jourdan; **132** Hospital de la Santa Creu I Sant Pau, AA/M Jourdan; **133** Hospital de la Santa Creu I Sant Pau, AA/M Jourdan; **134** Casa Batlló, AA/S L Day; **135** Casa Lleó-Morera, AA/M Chaplow; **136/7** Park Güell, AA/M Jourdan; **137** Park Güell, AA/M Jourdan; **138** Sagrada Família, AA/M Chaplow; **147** Cable car, Montjuïc, AA/S L Day; **148/9** Anella Olímpica, AA/M Chaplow; **149** Palau Sant Jordi, AA/S L Day; **150/1** Parc de l'Espanya Industrial, AA/S L Day; **150br** Parc de Joan Miró, Dona i Ocell, AA/M Jourdan; **151** Pavelló Mies van der Rohe, AA/M Jourdan; **152** Poble Espanyol, AA/M Jourdan; **155** Monestir de Pedralbes, AA/M Jourdan; **156/7** Monestir de Pedralbes, AA/M Jourdan; **156** Panels, Monestir de Pedralbes, AA/M Jourdan; **157** Museu del Futbol, Camp Nou Stadium, AA/M Chaplow; **158** Palau Reial de Pedralbes, AA/P Enticknap; **159** Parc d'Atraccions, AA/M Chaplow; **162/3** Girona, AA/M Chaplow; **165** Teatre-Museu Dalí, AA/M Chaplow; **166** Girona, AA/M Chaplow; **166/7** Hostalric, Girona, AA/M Chaplow; **168** Montserrat, AA/P Enticknap; **169** Black Virgin statue, Montserrat, AA/S Watkins; **170/1** Museum of Wine, Vilafranca de Peneses, AA/P Wilson; **172/3** Vilafranca de Penedes, AA/P Wilson; **174/5** Sitges, AA/S Watkins; **176** Tarragona, AA/P Enticknap; **177** Tarragona, AA/P Enticknap; **178/9** Cathedral, Tarragona, AA/P Enticknap.

Every effort has been made to trace the copyright holders, and we apologise in advance for any accidental errors. We

Street Index

Raset, Carrer de **5C**
Raval, Rambla del **19K**
R Batlle, Carrer **4C**
R Bonnat, Carrer **5E**
R Calvo, Carrer **6B**
R d'Escuder, Carrer **1F**
R de Castro, Carrer **11E**
Rector Triadó, Carrer del **16H**
Rector Ubach, Carrer **6D**
Regàs, Carrer **7E**
Regomir, Carrer **3d**
Rei Marti, Carrer **14G**
Reina d'Aragó **2F**
Reina E de Montcada, Passeig **3B**
Reina M Cristina, Avinguda de la **16J**
Reina Victòria, Carrer **5D**
Rei, Plaça del **4c**
Remei, Carrer del **3D**
Repartidor, Carrer **9C**
Republica Argentina, Avinguda de la **8C**
Reus, Carrer **6B**
Ribes, Carrer de **22J**
Ricart, Carrer de **16J**
Riego, Carrer **15G**
Riera Alta, Carrer de la **18J**
Riera de Tena, Carrer **13G**
Riereta, Carrer de la **18J**
Rios, Carrer **7C**
Riu de l'Or, Carrer **3C**
Rius i Taulet, Avinguda de **15J**
R Miquel i Planas, Carrer de **3A**
Robador, Carrer **19K**
Robi, Carrer del **8D**
Robrenyo, Carrer de **3F**
Rocafort, Carrer de **4F**
Roger, Carrer de **1E**
Roger de Flor, Carrer de **10F**
Roger de Llúria, Carrer de **21H**
Roma, Avinguda de **16G**
Roman Macaya, Carrer **7A**
Rosari, Carrer del **4C**
Ros de Olano, Carrer **8E**
Roser, Carrer del **17K**
Rosés, Carrer de **2F**
Rosselló, Carrer del **4F**
Rossend Arús, Carrer **14H**
Roura, Carrer de **6A**
R Sensat, Carrer **24L**
Rubens, Carrer de **9B**

Sabino de Arana, Carrer **2D**
Sagrat Cor, Carrer **4A**
Sagués, Carrer de **6E**
Sagunt, Carrer de **13G**
Salvà, Carrer **17K**

Salvat Papasseit, Passeig de **22L**
Samaniego, Carrer **10A**
Sancho de Avila, Carrer **23J**
Sanjoanistes, Carrer **7D**
Santa Agata, Carrer **8D**
Santa Albina, Carrer **10A**
Santa Amèlia, Carrer de **3C**
Santa Anna, Carrer **2a**
Santa Carolina, Carrer **11E**
Santa Catalina, Carrer **2F**
Santa Fe de Nou Mexic, Carrer **5D**
Santa Joana d'Arc, Carrer **12B**
Santaló, Carrer de **6E**
Santa Madrona, Passeig de **16K**
Sant Antoni Maria Claret, Carrer de **9F**
Sant Antoni, Ronda de **18J**
Santa Otilia, Carrer **11B**
Santa Rosa, Carrer **8D**
Santa Rosalia, Carrer **10A**
Sant Carles, Carrer **21L**
Sant Crispi, Carrer **10A**
Sant Crist, Carrer del **14G**
Sant Eudald, Carrer **9B**
Sant Fructuós, Carrer de **14H**
Sant Genis a Horta, Cami de **12A**
Sant Gervasi de Cassoles, Carrer **6B**
Sant Gervasi, Passeig de **7B**
Sant Jaume, Plaça de **3c**
Sant Joan Bosco, Passeig de **4C**
Sant Joan de la Salle, Carrer **6A**
Sant Joan, Passeig de **22H**
Sant Pau, Carrer de **18K**
Sant Pau, Ronda de **18K**
Sant Pere mès Baix, Carrer **21J**
Sant Pere Mitjà, Carrer **21J**
Sant Pere, Ronda de **20H**
Sant Quinti, Carrer de **1F**
Sants, Carrer de **1F**
Santuari, Carrer del **10B**
Santuari Sant Josep de la Muntanya, Avinguda **9D**
Saragossa, Carrer de **7C**
Sardenya, Carrer de **10E**
Sarrià, Avinguda de **4D**
Secretari Coloma, Carrer del **10E**
Segimon, Carrer **11B**
Segura, Carrer del **13J**
Seneca, Carrer **7F**
Septimània, Carrer **7D**

Sepúlveda, Carrer de **17H**
Sèrbia, Carrer **12D**
Sicilia, Carrer de **10F**
Sigüenza, Carrer de **11B**
Siracusa, Carrer **8E**
S Mundi, Carrer **4B**
Solá, Carrer de **3E**
Sor Eulàlia d'Anzizu, Carrer **1B**
Sors, Carrer de **9D**
Sostres, Carrer de **9C**
St Antoni, Carrer **2F**
St Cugat del Vallès, Carrer **9C**
St Elies, Carrer de **7D**
St Eusebi, Carrer de **7D**
St Germà, Carrer **15H**
St Gregori Taumaturg, Plaça **5D**
St Guillem, Carrer **7D**
St Hermen, Carrer **8D**
St Joaquim, Carrer **8E**
St Jordi, Carrer **1F**
St Lluis, Carrer de **9E**
St Magi, Carrer **8D**
St Marc, Carrer **7E**
St Màrius, Carrer de **6C**
St Medir, Carrer **1F**
St Miquel, Riera de **8E**
St Rafael, Carrer de **18K**
St Roc, Carrer **15H**
St Salvador, Carrer de **9D**
Sugranyes, Carrer de **1F**

Tallers, Carrer dels **19H**
Tamarit, Carrer de **17J**
Tànger, Carrer de **24J**
Tapioles, Carrer de **17K**
Taquigraf Garriga, Carrer del **3E**
Taquigraf Serra, Carrer **4E**
Tarragona, Carrer de **16H**
Tavern, Carrer de **6D**
T del Remei, Carrer **9B**
Telègraf, Carrer del **12D**
Tenerife, Carrer **11D**
Tenor Massini, Carrer del **2F**
Tenor Viñas, Carrer del **5E**
Teodora Lamadrid, Carrer **7B**
Teodor Roviralta, Carrer de **7A**
Terol, Carrer **8E**
Tetuan, Plaça de **22H**
T Flomesta, Carrer **1F**
Thous, Carrer de **11D**
Tibidabo, Avinguda del **7B**
Ticià, Carrer de **8A**
Tigre, Carrer de **19J**
Til lers, Passeig dels **2C**
Tinent Coronel Valenzuela, Carrer del **1C**
Tirso, Carrer **10B**

Toledo, Carrer **14G**
Tolrà, Carrer **12B**
Topazi, Carrer **8D**
Tòquio, Carrer **2C**
Tordera, Carrer de **8F**
Torras i Pujalt, Carrer **6C**
Torrent d'En Vidalet, Carrer del **9E**
Torrent de l'Olla, Carrer del **8F**
Torrent de les Flors, Carrer **9E**
Torres, Carrer **8F**
Torrijos, Carrer **9E**
Trafalgar, Carrer de **21J**
Tres Senyores, Carrer **9D**
Tres Torres, Carrer de les **4C**
Trias i Giró, Carrer **1C**
Trilla, Carrer **8D**
Tuset, Carrer **7E**

Universitat, Plaça de la **19H**
Universitat, Ronda **19H**

València, Carrer de **16G**
Valero, Carrer dels **5D**
Valladolid, Carrer de **2F**
Valldoncella, Carrer **19H**
Valldoreix, Carrer **9C**
Vallespir, Carrer de **3F**
Vallfogona, Carrer **8E**
Vallirana, Carrer de **7C**
Vallmajor, Carrer de **5D**
Valseca, Carrer **11D**
Varsòvia, Carrer de **12D**
Veciana, Carrer **9A**
Vell del Coll, Cami **11B**
Vendrell, Carrer **7A**
Verdi, Carrer de **9D**
Vergós, Carrer dels **4C**
Viada, Carrer **8D**
Via, Ronda de la **13G**
Vico, Carrer de **5C**
Viladomat, Carrer de **5F**
Vila i Vilà, Carrer de **18K**
Vilamari, Carrer de **16H**
Vilamur, Carrer **3E**
Vilardell, Carrer **15G**
Villafranca, Carrer **9D**
Villarroel, Carrer de **6F**
Vint-i-sis de Gener, Carrer **15H**
Violant d'Hongria, Carrer **1E**
Viriat, Carrer de **3F**
Vista Bella, Carrer de **6A**

Watt, Carrer **15G**
Wellington, Carrer de **23L**

Xifré, Carrer de **12F**

Zamora, Carrer de **24K**

Dear Reader

Your comments, opinions and recommendations are very important to us. Please help us to improve our travel guides by taking a few minutes to complete this simple questionnaire.

You do not need a stamp (unless posted outside the UK). If you do not want to cut this page from your guide, then photocopy it or write your answers on a plain sheet of paper.

Send to: **The Editor, AA World Travel Guides,**
FREEPOST SCE 4598, Basingstoke RG21 4GY.

Your recommendations...
We always encourage readers' recommendations for restaurants, nightlife or shopping – if your recommendation is used in the next edition of the guide, we will send you a **FREE AA Guide** of your choice from this series. Please state below the establishment name, location and your reasons for recommending it.

_____
_____
_____
_____
_____

Please send me **AA Guide** _____

About this guide...
Which title did you buy?
AA _____
Where did you buy it?_____
When? m m / y y
Why did you choose this guide? _____
_____
_____
_____
_____

Did this guide meet your expectations?

Exceeded ☐   Met all ☐   Met most ☐   Fell below ☐

Were there any aspects of this guide that you particularly liked? _____
_____
_____
_____

continued on next page...

Is there anything we could have done better? _____

_____

_____

_____

About you...

Name (*Mr/Mrs/Ms*) _____

Address _____

_____

_____ Postcode

Daytime tel nos _____

Email _____

Please only give us your mobile phone number or email if you wish to hear from us about other products and services from the AA and partners by text or mms, or email.

Which age group are you in?

Under 25 ☐   25–34 ☐   35–44 ☐   45–54 ☐   55–64 ☐   65+ ☐

How many trips do you make a year?

Less than one ☐   One ☐   Two ☐   Three or more ☐

Are you an AA member? Yes ☐   No ☐

About your trip...

When did you book? m m / ɏ ɏ   When did you travel? m m / ɏ ɏ

How long did you stay? _____

Was it for business or leisure? _____

Did you buy any other travel guides for your trip? _____

If yes, which ones? _____

_____

_____

Thank you for taking the time to complete this questionnaire. Please send it to us as soon as possible, and remember, you do not need a stamp (*unless posted outside the UK*).

AA Travel Insurance call 0800 072 4168 or visit www.theAA.com

---